The
Environment
of
Law
Enforcement

Prentice-Hall
Essentials of Law Enforcement Series
James D. Stinchcomb
Series Editor

DEFENSE AND CONTROL TACTICS
Georges Sylvain

ELEMENTS OF CRIMINAL INVESTIGATION
Paul B. Weston and Kenneth M. Wells

THE ENVIRONMENT OF LAW ENFORCEMENT
Victor G. Strecher

HANDBOOK OF COURTROOM DEMEANOR
AND TESTIMONY
C. Alex Pantaleoni

HANDBOOK OF VICE CONTROL
Denny F. Pace

PATROL OPERATIONS
Paul M. Whisenand and James L. Cline

POLICE-COMMUNITY RELATIONS
Alan Coffey, Edward Eldefonso,
and Walter Hartinger

YOUTH PROBLEMS AND LAW ENFORCEMENT
Edward Eldefonso

The
Environment
of
Law
Enforcement

A COMMUNITY RELATIONS GUIDE

VICTOR G. STRECHER
Michigan State University

PRENTICE-HALL, INC.
Englewood Cliffs, N.J.

P 13–283234–8
C 13–283242–9
Library of Congress Catalog Card Number: 70–151093
Printed in the United States of America

Current printing (last digit):
10 9 8 7 6 5 4 3 2 1

PRENTICE-HALL INTERNATIONAL, INC., *London*
PRENTICE-HALL OF AUSTRALIA PTY. LTD., *Sydney*
PRENTICE-HALL OF CANADA LTD., *Toronto*
PRENTICE-HALL OF INDIA PRIVATE LIMITED, *New Delhi*
PRENTICE-HALL OF JAPAN, INC., *Tokyo*

1/5/79 Becker Taylor 3.50

Introduction

Surely nothing can be more fundamental to guaranteeing the delivery of professional services than the employment of properly trained personnel. In pursuit of that goal, law enforcement officers and those who train them have long recognized the need for concise yet thoroughly documented information, well-researched and accurately presented.

In recent years, several commendable efforts have resulted in the availability of some valuable training resources. But too few of these were professionally developed by the textbook publishing companies, although their assistance was becoming imperative. The Prentice-Hall Essentials of Law Enforcement Series has been developed following a conference of national authorities who were asked to determine topics for priority production. The subject areas chosen are both timely and critical to the police and to their own increased determination to improve their service.

The potential use for this series is limited only by the creative imaginations of those responsible for peace officers' access to learning. Each book may perform as a supplement to a college course, as a resource for a training program, or as a reader to encourage informal study. It is the hope and the intent of the publisher, the editor, and the authors that these practical texts will contribute to the continuing progress being achieved by the nation's police.

James D. Stinchcomb

Institute for Justice
and Law Enforcement
Washington, D.C.

For Barbara, my wife

Policemen work in a variety of settings—territorial, social, and organizational—all of which influence their way of life and work. These settings include the police occupational structure and its traditions; the region of law enforcement operations (for most policemen the large city); the broad, enveloping social system and its forces of change; and the intergroup relations of everyday work. It is feasible to think of these settings, in their compounded form, as the total *environment of law enforcement*.

Ordinarily a police officer works for several years before he sorts out his individual impressions of his working world, and begins to make sense of them. Some officers eventually understand their environment very well, and most officers comprehend certain parts of it, but many others cannot resolve the apparent ambiguities and contradictions in their working lives, and tend to grasp a narrow edge of the reality. To the present, there has been no broadly available resource for officers who feel a need to understand more of their total working situation. In this sense police training has failed to satisfy a fundamental need.

This small book is a sampling of perspectives which might provide the police officer or student of law enforcement a running start toward understanding his social, organizational, and physical surroundings. It is an attempt to present information which is generally not included in the traditions and folklore learned from the previous generation of policemen. Many police officers grow into their work viewing contemporary events as unique and unprecedented. Their experience of social change is painfully intensified by its isolation from a historical context. Reduction of the tensions generated by these current conditions is a major objective of this book.

Acknowledgement of implicit assistance is due virtually

all of my associates and students; we continue to unfold each others' minds. More deeply and directly I am indebted to H. Sam Priest, Bill Hardin, and Edith McQuitty, who respectively created, developed, and currently directs the Library of the St. Louis Metropolitan Police Department, probably the finest law enforcement library to be found, anywhere. The end of their influence over the minds of policemen is nowhere in sight.

Contents

The Environment of Law Enforcement

Introduction

This book is for and about the policeman who is working in the community and for the young man or woman who is pursuing studies in criminal justice with the intention of working in law enforcement. It has little to do with the management perspective of the law enforcement environment, which has a typically institutional orientation, and which rarely reflects the individual view.

It is possible to consider the community and the other components of the environment from the perspective of the individual policeman rather than of the police organization. This shift in perspective produces a quite different set of considerations from those found at the departmental level. For one thing, only the individual officer knows firsthand what is really occurring in all parts of the police environment; police executives who administer on the basis of personal experience are inherently several years out of date, and those who rely upon reports from subordinates are using filtered, subjective information to guide their policy decisions. Another aspect of perspective is that administrative judgments of departmental goal accomplishment and each officer's evaluation of successful performance are likely to differ in several respects. Pressures upon the policeman differ from those influencing the chief of police, and their interpretations of the department's goals and strategies reflect this difference, even though most chiefs began their careers as policemen.

The patrolman's most pressing need is to successfully perform the duties expected of him, either on his own initiative or via radio dispatch. His success in performing these duties will have much to do with his career development in the department. But "success" can be interpreted in a variety of ways, and the criteria of success change over a period of

chapter

1

time. When a police recruit first enters the department, he is literally deluged by new sensory impressions, ranging from simple but new sounds and the feel of new physical exertions to strange and complex ideas. As any new employee would be, the police recruit is eager to please; he wants to succeed. In part deliberately, but to a greater extent casually and naturally, he discovers what is expected of him, and he delivers. But he also discovers that the expectations, coming from many points within the department, are sometimes contradictory and inconsistent. If there is a formal training program, the recruit may learn policy and procedure, only to be told by his sergeant or associates, after graduation, to forget the academic approach and to settle down to learning real police work on the streets. At other times, he will find disagreement between the expectations of his sergeant and his first few senior patrolmen partners. When this occurs, the recruit almost unconsciously considers the consequences of aligning himself with one of the conflicting positions, and often he also considers the difficult challenge of maintaining a neutral position. He may gradually align his interpretations of his new work and of the world about him to one faction or another because of strong feelings of *practicality* (a desire to avoid conflict with strong factions); *loyalty* (to an early partner or supervisor); *idealism* (acceptance of a nonpopular view); *subordination* (response to a strong leader); or any number of other personal drives. An alternative is to remain aloof from these pulls upon his loyalties and to become a "loner."

All of this is part of learning a new role—that of the *police officer*—and the recruit once again feels the pressures of having to meet expectations similar to those of childhood and adolescence. He experiences again the uncertainties caused by half-understood traditions, demanding details of appropriate behavior, and the fear and shame of blunder. Most recruits enter this role-learning situation poorly prepared to exercise sound judgment as the various alternatives are thrust upon them. Indeed, few occupations demand of their practitioners that they make up their minds about so many crucial issues so quickly. Recruitment to police work is enticing, training is short, and on-the-job internships are intensive. Full membership as an associate depends upon fulfilling the appropriate role. It is difficult for a new policeman to maintain a clear perspective under these conditions and to develop any real comprehension of his community, his organization's community function, and his individual role within those larger systems.

In one sense at least, all training is designed to narrow the range of a man's behavior when he is confronted with certain conditions; for example, so that the organization will have some stability, all policemen are expected to react in the same general way when called by the radio dispatcher. This necessary narrowing of responses often has the undesirable side effect of narrowing perceptions as well—of producing tunnel vision. When this effect becomes acute in an individual, he is unlikely to understand much of what occurs outside his immediate work setting. In a sense, he resembles those ancients who viewed the earth as the center of the universe, who saw the sun, air, sea, and stars as materials organized for their personal benefit. There are some police officers who view all of society as being organized around the law enforcement function, who cannot distinguish between social control as a necessity for broader social functioning and social control as the central function of the social system.

Such blind spots might have little significance in the work of a machinist or a chemical engineer, men who deal with nonliving materials. But it is no exaggeration to say that the entire quality of a policeman's performance might well depend upon his understanding of the police function, of its settings, and of his relationship with others.

This book is, in fact, an effort to provide a few aids to the perspective of the young man engaged in police work or just entering the field. It is based upon the author's conviction that a policeman will have difficulty understanding his job until he clearly understands: (1) the origins of his job—the historical development of law enforcement; (2) how his work setting became what it is—the evolution of our cities; (3) what the social system is and how it got this way—the nature of change; (4) collective behavior among groups—labels and efficiency; and (5) the individual policeman's place among these large-scale forces—his capacity for influence and effectiveness on a daily basis.

This is not to say that a policeman needs to be a historian, urbanologist, sociologist, and psychologist merely to understand his role and to better perform his work. It is more accurate to say that each of these large disciplines contains material which bears directly upon the policeman's work, upon his very existence, and that to ignore them is to work in the dark. Each of the following chapters deals with one of these slices of perspective, which we hope will enable the police officer to, in the old mariner's phrase, "keep his eyes on the mast and the stars at the same time."

The
Policeman
As
Proxy

In an effort to gain perspective on the police function and the policeman's role, we might ask questions about the origin of law enforcement, and we might ask directly: What is the police job? What is a policeman, and who does he work for?

A universal need, one which takes its place beside the needs for shelter, food, and human association, is the requirement of personal safety and security. It is difficult to go about one's ordinary day-to-day activities in an atmosphere of uncertainty, intimidation, or fear. And without exception, history shows that interpersonal violence and disregard for the property rights of others have existed as disruptive forces in every society. The containment of human conflict and the maintenance of at least minimal social order have been concerns of even the earliest, most primitive societies if anthropological studies and ancient folklore are acceptable indicators.

From Primitive to Formal
Social Controls

In order to give some sense of the historical progression of law enforcement, the long era of human existence on earth has been cut down to a manageable size in Table 1. The 20,000 years during which man has been around in his present form have been compressed into the 365 days of a single year, as if *homo sapiens* appeared in his cave on January 1, and progressed to the present time, December 31. Much like time-lapse photography, 20,000 years = 365 days; 100 years of

chapter

2

JAN. FEB. MAR. APR. MAY JUNE JULY AUG. SEPT. OCT. NOV. DEC.

Man appeared on earth; evolved through family, clan, tribal groupings; developed agriculture. (18,000–6000 B.C.)

Sumerian ships used Tigris and Euphrates rivers. (7000 B.C.)

Sumerian farming and irrigation. (6500 B.C.)

Ubaid, oldest known city, in Mesopotamia. (4000 B.C.)

Egyptians mapped the stars, developed 12 signs of the zodiac. (3000 B.C.)

CODE OF HAMMURABI, OLDEST KNOWN WRITTEN LAW. (2100 B.C.)

Phoenician shipping on the Mediterranean Sea. (2000 B.C.)

TEN COMMANDMENTS. (1800 B.C.)

EGYPTIAN COURTS; MARINE PATROL. (1500–1400 B.C.)

Carthage founded. (800 B. C.)

Rome built. (753 B.C.)

Confucius born in China (551 B.C.)

Buddha born in India. (550 B.C.)

Plato lived in Greece. (387 B.C.)

Alexander the Great conquered Egypt. (332 B.C.)

Evidence of use of writing, arithmetic, money, military horses.

PRAETORIAN GUARD AND VIGILES FOR INTERNAL SECURITY IN ROME. (27 B.C.)

Christ born.

Establishment of "official" Christianity. (325 A.D.)

Fall of Rome. (395 A.D.)

Span of Dark Ages in Europe. (400–900 A.D.)

HUE AND CRY COMMUNITY PROTECTION IN ENGLAND. (600 A.D.)

CREATION OF ENGLISH SHERIFFS AND CONSTABLES. (700 A.D.)

CHARLEMAGNE'S LAWS PROCLAIMED. (785 A.D.)

Columbus landed in the West Indies. (1492 A.D.)

Ponce de León discovered Florida. (1513 A.D.)

Copernicus challenged earth-center-of-universe theory. (1543 A.D.)

BRUNO BURNED BY THE CHURCH FOR ADVOCACY OF COPERNICUS' THEORY. (1600)

First Englishmen landed in North America. (1602)

FIRST PENAL COLONY IN AMERICA; CRIMINALS EXILED TO VIRGINIA. (1617)

First slaves, 20 Negroes, arrived in Virginia. (1619)

ENACTMENT OF BLUE LAWS IN VIRGINIA; DRESS ACCORDING TO RANK. (1619)

Pilgrims reached Plymouth on the *Mayflower*. (1620)

FIRST INDIAN MASSACRE OF COLONISTS OUTSIDE JAMESTOWN. (1622)

VIRGINIA LAW EXEMPTS "PERSONS OF QUALITY" FROM PENAL WHIPPING. (1623)

Purchase of Manhattan Island by Peter Minuit. (1626)

Fifteen-hundred children kidnapped in Europe and sold in Virginia. (1627)

Boston founded. (1630)

FIRST CRIMINAL EXECUTION IN PILGRIM COLONY. (1630)

Great migration to Massachusetts; only 4,000 of 16,000 church members. (1630–40)

MASSACHUSETTS LAW LIMITS CITIZENSHIP RIGHTS TO CHURCH MEMBERS (1631)

First tavern opened in Boston. (1634)

Harvard College founded. (1636)

6

DECEMBER—expanded

24th 25th 26th 27th 28th 29th 30th

New Amsterdam Governor estimated more than one quarter of buildings were "grog shops." (1637)
Twenty different nationalities and sects on Manhattan Island, speaking 18 languages. (1643)
First colonial labor organization, Shoemakers of Boston. (1648)
FIRST AMERICAN POLICE FORCE: *RATEL-WACHT* IN NEW AMSTERDAM. (1658)
Declaration of Independence. (1776)
United States 5% urban, 95% rural. (1790)
Population of earth reaches ONE BILLION, after almost 20,000 years of growth. (1820)
TEXAS RANGERS BECOME FIRST STATE POLICE ORGANIZATION. (1835)
United States 11% urban, 89% rural. (1840)
NEW YORK CITY POLICE DEPARTMENT FORMED. (1845)
Charles Darwin published *ORIGIN OF SPECIES*. (1859)
BERTILLON SYSTEM OF PERSONAL IDENTIFICATION USED BY POLICE (1879)
BULLET IDENTIFICATION WITH SPECIFIC GUN BY LAND-AND-GROOVE MARKS. (1889)
United States 35% urban, 65% rural. (1890)
HENRY SYSTEM OF FINGERPRINT CLASSIFICATION INTRODUCED. (1896)
Highest population density in Western world—New York City (East Side): 350,000/sq. mile. (1900)
FIRST USE OF MOUNTED POLICE: NEW YORK CITY. (1904)
First successful airplane flight by Wright brothers. (1904)
Einstein published First General Theory of Relativity. (1905)
F.B.I. ESTABLISHED. (1908)
First wireless message from New York City to Chicago. (1909)
Barney Oldfield drove 133 MPH at Daytona Beach. (1910)
Discovery of vitamins. (1912)
Ford's first assembly line introduced. (1913)
Outbreak of World War I. (1914)
F.B.I. REORGANIZED UNDER J. E. HOOVER. (1924)
EARLIEST KNOWN USE OF RADIOS IN POLICE CARS. (1929)
Population of earth reaches TWO BILLION, doubles in 110 years. (1930)
United States 57% urban, 43% rural. (1940)
Outbreak of World War II. (1939)
First nuclear bomb detonated. (1945)
United States 70% urban, 30% rural. (1960)
Population of earth reaches THREE BILLION. (1965)

7

history = 1 day, 19 hours, 41 minutes; 1 year = 26.3 minutes. This simple technique of time compression makes it possible to grasp the broad implications of historic social evolution, without being blinded by single events. It also has the effect of highlighting the cumulative effects of our historical development, pointing up the acceleration and rising momentum of change.

In this long year of man's history, most of the first six months were spent in a gradual transition from single family groups living in natural shelters, to multifamily clans, and then into tribes. Some of these tribes lived by hunting, fishing, and gathering wild edible plants; others moved about less, and evolved and practiced agriculture, including irrigation, by about July 29 (6500 B.C.).

The first written laws of conduct, the Code of Hammurabi, did not appear until eighteen days into the last quarter of man's life on earth—the quarter which continues to our present time. (It is interesting to note that the signs of the zodiac were created by the Egyptians prior to this first written law.) The Ten Commandments followed the Code of Hammurabi by six of our compressed days.

Prior to these first recorded rules of behavior, social control was largely a matter of strong leadership within small groups—at first the leadership of the father, later of the clan patriarch, then the tribal chief. Because these relatively small groupings existed in harsh, hostile environments for the most part, survival depended to a large extent upon internal cooperation and individual responsibility under stern leadership. Most of the danger to the group was external, in the form of competing families, clans, and tribes, and wild animals; competition was for the scarce goods of survival: food, natural shelter, fuel. However, external threats to survival became magnified and often lethal when internal controls broke down; squabbling, factionalized tribes easily succumbed to unified, well-led tribes. Thus, from the earliest days internal and external security have been vitally related.

In a sense, the code of behavior within a group, whether formal and written or tacitly understood folklore, is a kind of personal bargain for each group member, whereby he accepts restrictions upon his behavior in exchange for personal security. It is seldom a consciously made bargain, but more of a narrow high-ground path between quicksand and the cliff and to escape the pressures and controls of the group,

The Policeman As Proxy

one would have to accept a more lonely and desperate fate outside.

However, just as modern man spends much less time in survival-related activity than did his ancestors, modern man's variety of social life is less restricted by security considerations than previously. The size, the great variety of beliefs, the speed of mass communications, and the unprecedented self-consciousness of our society have combined to dislocate the old conformity-security bargain. Nothing in modern life is any longer so simple, even though many citizens cling to old patterns with fearful hopes that they will be the safer for it. But the forms of human group living have passed through many phases—from primitive to the present—before reaching this state of complexity. This pattern of change and its implications for the policeman will be dealt with not only in this chapter but also in the next two.

It was not long after the Code of Hammurabi and the Ten Commandments were set forth that the Egyptians found it necessary to initiate courts to administer the law and, soon thereafter, policing operations in the form of harbor patrols and customs enforcement units. This ancient pattern of institutional support for rules is significant for us even today, for it appears to be an established sequence of social development, much discussed by social scientists interested in the progression from primitive to industrial societies. Differences between early and recent forms of social control have been expressed in pairs of concepts by numerous theorists: primitive-modern, folk-urban, *gemeinschaft-gesellschaft*, organic-mechanical, sacred-secular, moral-legal, and familial-institutional. At one time all human society could be described as follows:

Simple—Having little social class differentiation and strong personal bonds among its members
Small—Covering a small territory
Consensual—Showing agreement on moral issues
Relatively unspecialized—Having few institutions, a premoney economy, and little occupational specialization

Human society progressed from these primitive features toward current modes of living, which are characterized as:

Complex—Having several classes, castes, or strata; more impersonal, businesslike relationships

The Policeman As Proxy

Large—In population; covering a large geographic territory

Rational—Having explicit rules and regulations instead of moral consensus as a guide to behavior; numerous institutions designed to "administer" relationships among people, while previously moral agreements sufficed

✳ *Specialized*—Having a complex economy with a symbolic medium of exchange; very few families able to provide for all their own needs

Society's progression from its simple primitive to its complex modern form has been clearly discernible in the evolution of social control. With this in mind, it is clear that a historical perspective of law enforcement cannot begin with a look at the 1658 *ratel-wacht* in New Amsterdam. Although this first American police department makes *law enforcement* a very *young occupation* in the New World, it is more useful to observe that *social control* is one of the *oldest functions* in the world as a whole. Those who would trace modern law enforcement to its occupational ancestors—Peel's London bobbies, the English sheriff, the Roman Vigiles, or others— fail entirely to trace the *social function* through history because of their tight focus on outwardly similar processes, titles, or offices. They would have us accept the notion that police work began when laws were written down for the first time.

Perhaps the reverse way of looking at that sequence is more accurate. To consider that writing the law and making adherence to this formal body of law—with all its strategies and specialization—a rational matter took away much of the power of moral consensus. Moral agreement lost this power when the interpretation of right and wrong became a specialized occupation and judgments were made by a trained few rather than by a strong leader or the community at large.

But social forms do not die easily; and the total social group continues to practice moral judgments, although moral agreement is present only in small subgroups rather than in the whole society. What our complex modern society has brought us, then, is a double system of social control. On the one hand, we have the system built upon law—and a rationalized system which spells out relationships among people in terms of legal obligations and expectations. This system is served by a secular priesthood which, by its own claim, is solely qualified to interpret questions of legality—and, thus, of acceptable human conduct. Organized around this body

The Policeman As Proxy

of law and its practitioners is a system of institutions (legislative, executive, judicial, professional), which provides a medium of expression for the law and the means for carrying out its processes. This system of institutions reserves to itself all lasting judgments.

On the other hand, the people who constitute the society continue to make moral evaluations of all others around them, on the basis of whatever moral code they hold valid. Frequently their moral judgments do not agree with those of the legal system, or as often, their judgments seem to agree with the legal system, but the legal priesthood engages in little-understood strategies that seem to sidestep the consequences of immorality. These parallel systems—the rationalized legal-institutional structure and the community moral evaluation process—coexist, but in a state of increasing discomfort.

All of this, however, has happened only in the last few days of history, using our compressed year. It is worth noting that the first nine and one-half months of man's historical year were required to get out of the cave, to learn farming and boatbuilding, and to grow beyond the family unit in social organization. The next one and one-half months, or 46 days, witnessed a social revolution which encompassed the Ten Commandments; the building of Carthage and Rome; the births of Confucius, Buddha, Plato, Socrates, Alexander the Great, and Christ; and then the fall of Rome and the onset of the Dark Ages in Europe. This was the first great epoch of self-consciousness, in which man extended his ability to stand off from himself and philosophize about the meaning of existence. However, the philosophy of that period never overcame its early turning inward, its fatal tendency to seek all answers by reasoning logically about the nature of objects, without bothering to *look at those objects before reasoning about them*. Thus it was possible for Aristotle to describe a right-angle trajectory for a rock-missile, when observation and measurement would have forced his logic in another, more valid direction. It is ironic that because of this simple flaw, such great and wonderful minds remained prescientific and unable to break through the surface of reality.

It was during this same period that the first *institutions* of social control originated and grew. When man crept out of the cave, he discovered that internal group control did not take care of itself; and after centuries of strong personal leadership in small groups, he discovered that for maintaining direct control, one man's attention did not extend sufficiently through time to cover the twenty-four hours or through space to cover territory beyond his vision. The designation of chieftains and subordinate leaders eventually led to more elaborate organizational structures and, incidentally, to much of the organizational folklore which is still taught in our day: unity of command, span of control, chain of command, and other concepts.

Though mere speculation, it is probable that the first *institutional* means of social control were offshoots of military operations redirected inward to put down challenges to tribal leadership. The Roman Praetorian Guard and Vigiles, with their focus on internal control and security, constituted a departure from the all-purpose military force. But we make a fundamental error in searching for the ancestors of American law enforcement agencies among these early forms of internal security. Although we can go back to the Ten Commandments and, some centuries after, to early institutionalized forms of law enforcement—the Egyptian customs officers, harbor patrols, and courts; later the Roman Praetorian Guard and Vigiles; and then the English constables and sheriffs—it is much more difficult to trace a true developmental path to our present-day American law enforcement scene. In fact, to do so is perhaps to be blinded by the superficial similarities of function and method between the ancients and our current police, and at the same time, to be unmindful of the more significant and fundamental differences between them.

Those who trace the origins of our democratic governmental forms to ancient Greece should read again the works of Plato, which would decree the death penalty to those aspiring to an occupation or social status different from that of their father—the ones they were born to and frozen into. This merely suggests that we take a closer look at the similarities and differences between the social values and governmental forms of the past, and accept less readily the idea that modern policing is truly an offspring of similar ancient functions.

At the heart of this look at the past is man's relationship to his government or *leaders*. Ancient empires and monarchies generally considered the individual human being to be the property of the monarch and subject always to his will. Thus it was that suicide was considered a violation of the king's law, not on moral grounds but because suicide robbed the

The Policeman As Proxy

monarch of his rightful property—a living man. Concepts of governmental authority and power were based upon the divine right of a king to rule and upon the size of his army —neatly covering both the sacred domain and the secular. The idea of a common electorate, a broad participation in the selection of governmental leaders, would have been unthinkable in those times. Even the colonists who came to America to escape oppression were not prepared to go the whole distance in popular government, as is seen in the 1631 decree of the Massachusetts General Court that only members of the established church would be extended the privilege of citizenship. This law, it should be noted, was passed during a ten-year wave of migration into Massachusetts, which saw 16,000 persons enter the colony, only 4,000 of whom were church members. Citizenship, for some time, was a minority privilege even in America.

American Law Enforcement as a Discontinuity

The powerful and dramatic events of the 1760s and 1770s, the American revolutionary era, forced to the surface of the colonial society a new concept of the individual's relationship to his government; true, the ideas of democracy had existed as fragments for a considerable period, but never before in so practicable a format. The salient fact to be derived from this beginning of our nation—for law enforcement—is the *shattering of continuity with past systems of social control*. In fact, the continuity with European and with earlier colonial police operations should have been shattered even more thoroughly and replaced by new modes of control better suited to the magnificent philosophy underlying the new government. But alternatives to European constables and sheriffs were not easily imagined, much less readily implemented in a struggling new democracy, and the old formats continued. Police functions in America, however, were never the same as for their predecessors, who maintained the monarch, collected his taxes, and kept the peasants in line. If some of these functions continued within American policing, to that extent our police system failed to meet the challenges and expectations of the great experiment in democracy. And

The Policeman As Proxy

despite the conversion of an inherited enforcement format to a new philosophy and practice, it is clear that the law enforcement requirements of the United States of America were unlike those of any previous government, anywhere in the world.

A question every policeman needs to ask himself—not just once, at the time he enters police work, but many times throughout his career—is whether he really believes in, and is committed to, the concepts of democracy and individual liberty. It is one thing to give a quick affirmative answer and then go about everyday practical matters, but it is quite another matter to consider all the duties, responsibilities, restraints, and complications which flow from that fundamental philosophical question. The logical consequences of a firm belief in our form of government make American policing more difficult and demanding than would a comparable allegiance to any other form of government. Why? Because our government was deliberately intended by its originators and early builders to have certain characteristics; as a result, the following can be said of it.

1. It is a rarity among world governments, in having declared itself willing to accept the broadest possible range of peoples, cultures, social classes, religions, values, and political beliefs. Fifteen years before the first police force was organized in 1658 (the *ratel-wacht*, or "rattlewatch," in New Amsterdam), there were 20 different nationalities and sects on Manhattan Island, speaking 18 languages.

2. Although social classes do exist in the United States, social scientists have been at pains to find another term to describe our layered society (for example, social "stratification," or "status") because our focus has never been upon fixed class membership but rather on movement upward in the system, that is, social "mobility." The vigor of this seething social milieu has led simultaneously to enormous growth and development and to social problems unmatched in other countries. From the beginning, aspirations and expectations have been high in America; they are still high. Yet in the best of systems, relatively few achieve all their goals, and for many others the goals continue to rise as they meet them, like a series of plateaus—always one more goal visible and attainable with just a little more effort. This open-ended medium of social mobility, of course, leads to great disappointments for (*a*) those who fail

The Policeman As Proxy

to achieve their original ambitions and (*b*) those whose goals are always a step ahead of their progress.

3. Our American culture is *self-conscious* in the sense that it has continuously monitored its progress toward the ideals set forth by its founders. Persons from the United States are considered by those from other countries to be refreshingly frank and open about their beliefs and their shortcomings, sometimes embarrassingly so. Also, they are pragmatic, outspoken, and not inclined toward compulsive law observance or subservience. These characteristics, of course, cannot be applied with uniformity to individual human beings, but they can be applied as generalizations about the American culture.

America was obviously not designed to make police work easy. But we might ponder whether most policemen would want to live in a country which maximizes controls over individual lives, in which police power holds the edge under all circumstances.

One of the questions posed at the beginning of this chapter was *Who does the policeman work for?* To answer this it is necessary only to compare our Constitution, Bill of Rights, and Declaration of Independence with the philosophies of previous governments. The conclusion is inescapable that in this country, perhaps for the first time in recorded history, *policemen are proxies for other citizens.* In our specialized society, work is divided; one man produces shoes for 1,000 families, one policeman maintains security for, perhaps, 500 individuals. Law enforcement in America is not the maintenance of a monarch, the suppression of popular opinion, or the protection of elites. It is every man's function of maintaining security of person and property, delegated to specialists—the policemen.

Cities That Nobody Planned

It is customary to think and talk of our cities as being in a state of decline—a state of general deterioration. Symptoms of urban decay most often described are crime in the streets, neighborhood deterioration and the spread of slums through property neglect; the increased incidence of vice violations—prostitution, gambling, and drugs; the displacement of neighborhood populations by in-migrants; juvenile delinquency; political dissent and social polarization; urban peace disturbances and major disorders; and a general lack of respect for the city government, particularly for the police.

This view of deteriorating cities is based upon an assumption that cities were formerly good and pleasant dwelling places—that it was safe to walk their streets, that people shared a calm passion for democracy, that morality was in charge, that patriotism was consensual, and that nice people lived in nice cities. Permit a challenge to this gargantuan assumption, and all its minor points as well, using documentation rather than opinion. It is not especially useful to say that crime, immorality, political disagreement, and slums have always been found in our big cities. This is generally known or assumed. What seems to escape most current observers is the *degree* to which these conditions were present in the cities of the past. The many reasons for a tendency to minimize past social problems and glamorize earlier times need not be analyzed except to say that fantasy provides a convenient platform for those who wish to express their discontent at growing older without the fulfillment of human perfection or even improvement.

What, then, were cities like a few generations ago? What was it like to be a policeman in 1900, 1850, 1800? What were the problems, and how were they handled? Probably the only way to gain insight into these matters is to sample the comments of observers. It is our good fortune that a number of competent persons considered it worthwhile to record in some detail the events which filled their days and that some of these observers had a primary interest in police affairs. From these old accounts it is possible to sketch an image of the large American city of a century ago and to use it as a kind of base line from which progress or a change for the worse may be estimated. Because this is not a general historical treatise, the focus will be upon community safety and law enforcement.

When It Was Safe to Walk the Streets

The nostalgic images of "Our Town," the "Gay Nineties," and the "Good Old Days," do us a disservice, portraying as they do cities and times which never existed for most ordinary citizens, and creating a yearning for which there is likely to be no remedy. For a policeman in these times of great change and turbulence, the vision of a calm community is especially attractive, and the temptation is strong to believe that a calm community once existed and could exist once again if only the right policies were adopted and appropriate actions taken. No doubt, pleasant small towns have existed, and life for their inhabitants may have been idyllic. But the city dwellers of past generations knew little of this, and the predominant environment of policing—the big city, the "crucible of culture"—has not differed significantly from what we experience today, as the following reports indicate.

*   *   *

"On August 7, 1892, after night, the St. Mary Market gang created a violent disturbance at the head of the market. . . .The arrival of the police on the scene was the signal for a fusillade of small-arms fire and the gallant corporal [policeman] fell mortally wounded. Joseph Johns, Donelson and Dennis Donahue were those who were convicted without capital punishment for his murder."[1]

[1]George W. Hale, *Police and Prison Cyclopaedia* (Boston: W. L. Richardson Co., 1893), pp. 341–42.

Omaha—1892. From the Report of the Chief of Police. ". . . the resident districts of Omaha usually have no police protection, and are left to the mercy of tramps, sneak thieves, burglars, house-breakers, veranda climbers, and other criminals, who, besides our local law breakers, are always well informed as to the localities that have no police protection."[2]

Boston—1756. "In consequence of numerous evening processions got up by the lower classes, and ending often in bloodshed, a law was passed to prevent such assemblages."[3]

Boston—1765. "Captain Semmes, of the South Watch, reported that 'Negro Dick came to the watchhouse, and reported rowdies under his window. Watchmen were sent, and met a gang of rowdies, one of which drew a sword. The watch cried murder and fled to the watchhouse, and the rowdies escaped.' "[4]

Boston—1769. "In consequence of existing difficulties, the watch were ordered 'to patrol two together.' "[5]

Chicago—1862. ". . . during the year . . . the city was infested with 'bad' men from all over the West. . . . There was also a co-terie of sluggers here, who were constantly creating disturbances and making trouble for the officers. . . . All along the east side of Market Street, from Van Buren to Madison streets, were located dozens of low-down dens and sailors' boarding houses, where broils and murders were of frequent occurrence. . . . From these dens came the seemingly endless crowd of bounty-jumpers and desperadoes, who at one time became so bold in their operations that respectable citizens proposed to organize a vigilance commit-tee for the purpose of clearing the city of these pestiferous and dangerous classes."[6]

Chicago—1880. ". . . the toughest district in the city was in the second precinct. . . . Within this area there existed the worst ele-ments in the city. Gangs of young hoodlums frequented the cor-ners and held up and beat passing pedestrians 'just for the fun

[2]Ibid., p. 354.

[3]Edward H. Savage, Police Records and Recollections, or Boston by Daylight and Gaslight for Two Hundred and Forty Years (Boston: John P. Dale & Co., 1873), pp. 29–30.

[4]Ibid., p. 31.

[5]Ibid., p. 33.

[6]John J. Flinn, History of the Chicago Police (Chicago: Police Book Fund, 1887), pp. 103–6.

Cities That Nobody Planned

of the thing,' and even made so bold occasionally as to attack a solitary policeman."[7]

Before Morality Had Decayed

Philadelphia—1697. William Penn, sixteen years after designing the city of Philadelphia, expressed his disappointment "That there is no place more overrun with wickedness and sins so very scandalous, openly committed in defiance of law and virtue. . . ."[8]

Boston—1816. "As respects *The Hill*, it consists principally of drunkards, harlots, spendthrifts, and outcasts from the country; in truth Beelzebub holds a court there, and almost every Town in the Commonwealth has a representative. These are great nuisances, but every large town has them . . . in spite of jails and workhouses, and probably will till the millennium."[9]

Boston—1823. " 'Shaking down,' by the girls, becomes frequent on The Hill. Mayor Quincy inaugurates stringent measures there."[10]

Boston—1851. "On the eve of the 23rd of April . . . we made the great Police descent in Ann Street, capturing some one hundred and sixty bipeds, who were punished for piping, fiddling, dancing, drinking, and attending crimes."[11]

Boston—1870. "The Police arrested 183 nightwalkers (night of May 7), most of whom were subsequently sent to their friends out of the city."[12]

In 1892 George W. Hale surveyed the police departments of the United States and several other countries, obtaining for the first time a great body of data regarding the administration of police departments and the prevalence of crime. Although the statistics were crude and undoubtedly

---

[7]*Ibid.*, p. 406.

[8]Charles N. Glaab, *The American City: A Documentary History* (Homewood, Ill.: Dorsey Press, 1963), p. 37.

[9]Savage, *Police Records and Recollections*, p. 57.

[10]Savage, *Police Records and Recollections*, p. 63.

[11]*Ibid.*, p. 90.

[12]*Ibid.*, p. 106.

inaccurate in many cases, they represented a significant step toward the establishment of uniform crime reports and information sharing among law enforcement agencies. On the subject of morality, Mr. Hale asked whether houses of prostitution existed in each of the jurisdictions queried, whether they were licensed, and what enforcement action was customarily taken. Following is a small sampling of verbatim replies of chiefs of police to his inquiry, published in 1893:[13]

Appleton, Wis. "Houses of prostitution are not licensed. There are 3 houses and 10 inmates. When they get 'foxy' we clean them out and allow a new crew to come in."

Atlanta, Ga. "Houses of prostitution are not licensed in this city. They are restricted to one locality as much as possible, and also required to comply with all police regulations."

Atlantic City, N.J. "Houses of prostitution are not licensed. There are about 10 houses, which average 6 inmates. I regulate them. So long as they are orderly they remain; if disorderly I raid their houses and drive them out of town. Knowing this, they do not give me much trouble."

Burlington, Iowa. "The houses of prostitution are pulled monthly. There are 4 houses and 18 inmates."

Dallas, Tex. "Houses of prostitution are not licensed. Twelve houses, and about 120 prostitutes. Monthly fines are assessed on the inmates."

Duluth, Minn. "There are 15 houses of prostitution, and 100 inmates. Keepers fined once a month, and oftener if they do not behave and keep orderly."

Evansville, Ind. "Houses of prostitution are not licensed, but are fined. The keepers go before the grand jurors every term of court and are prosecuted."

Fort Wayne, Ind. "Houses of prostitution are not licensed. Number of houses, 4; inmates, 24. They are arrested 4 times a year, and fined $15.50 each."

Jackson, Mich. "Houses of prostitution are not licensed. Cannot tell number; only know there are too many."

[13]Hale, *Police and Prison Cyclopaedia*, pp. 193–454.

Cities That Nobody Planned

Joliet, Ill. "There are no houses of prostitution. There are no rules or regulations on this subject, and we do not allow any such places in this city."

Kalamazoo, Mich. "No statistics on hand regarding houses of prostitution. Great plenty."

Leadville, Colo. "Houses of prostitution are licensed. There are about 50 houses and 200 inmates. No rules and regulations; only under the Chief of Police."

Lebanon, Pa. "Do not know anything about houses of prostitution in this moral community."

Memphis, Tenn. "Houses of prostitution are not licensed. Prostitutes must not be on the street after 9 P.M. Must not enter saloons, nor [go] carriage riding at night, nor flaunt their avocation at any time on the street. No minors to be admitted into their houses."

Milwaukee, Wis. "Houses of prostitution are not licensed. Number of known houses of ill-fame, 53; inmates, 175."

Minneapolis, Minn. "There are 22 licensed houses of prostitution, with 118 inmates. Keepers pay $50.00, and inmates $5.00 per month."

Norwich, Conn. "Houses of prostitution are not licensed. We had 7 houses broken up, and drove out all but 3. They are doing very little business."

Omaha, Nebr. "Houses of prostitution are not licensed, but keepers and inmates pay a monthly fine as follows: girls, $8.00; keepers, $28.00. There are 24 houses, and an average of 190 prostitutes."

St. Louis, Mo. "Houses of prostitution are not licensed. There are 259 houses of prostitution and assignation with about 900 inmates. There are no rules or regulations for them, but they are only allowed in two of the seven police districts of the city. If they go where they are not wanted, or if persons are robbed in their houses, or if they make themselves too conspicuous, they are arrested and fined for being 'keepers or inmates.' "

Savannah, Ga. "There are 10 recognized houses of prostitution in this city that may be called first-class of their kind. . . ."

Before Morality Had Decayed

Sioux City, Iowa. "There are 9 houses of prostitution. The madam pays $30.00 a month; the girls pay $10.00 a month."

For those who are inclined to equate sexual morality with the length of women's skirts, the sheer volume of sex for sale during the Victorian era must come as something of a surprise. This sampling of police chiefs' responses is representative of the range of their statements in the survey. All but a few forthrightly reported the existence of houses of prostitution within their jurisdictions. The tone of their replies ranges from resignation to vigorous and earthy pragmatism, with surprisingly few expressions of moral evaluation. Typically, the concerns of the chiefs centered upon orderliness, restriction of locality, cleanliness, prevention of related crimes of violence, and in general, inoffensiveness to the rest of the community.

There is an observable interplay among three categories of "information" about sexual behavior, and by extension, sexual morality. First, there is each person's *knowledge* of his own behavior, and perhaps that of an intimate friend or two. Second, there is each person's *belief* regarding the sexual activity of others, richly mixed with his own attitudes, wishes and fantasies about sex. And third, there is the *portrayal* of sexual behavior in the communications media: novels, films, magazines, plays, news, and other formats. These widely diffused representations consist not of a summation of the first category above—that is, a person's knowledge of his own behavior—but rather of the beliefs and fantasies of a small segment of the population: the creative intellectuals, who deal with ideas, images, and phrases.

It is customary to consider our times emancipated from many of the sexual taboos of previous generations, particularly Victorian taboos. The phrase "new morality" is most expressive of this popular belief, but there is much to suggest that the new morality is perhaps a mere avant-garde claim of changed moral status, rather than a genuine social trend. Certainly we have nothing to match the dispassionate reports of the police chiefs on prostitution in their own jurisdictions during the height of the Victorian era. If morality has decayed, it has not done so in recent times.

There are perhaps two interesting lessons to be learned from these fragmentary glimpses of the past. The first is that human values and customs cannot be understood in terms of

Cities That Nobody Planned

"past" and "present," as if these two terms sum up all of human experience. There are many pasts, and a rapidly changing present, all of which constitute cycles in cultural development. The second lesson is that our judgment of the state of morality, past and present, is compounded of very little factual information, some personal experience, and considerable opinion and speculation. For, as Masters and Johnson observed in their monumental work, *Human Sexual Response*,[14] our scientifically reliable knowledge of human sexual behavior—in both the social and physical sense—is considerably less than that concerning the sexual habits of virtually any other species of living thing.

The following extract from the 1892 report of the Chief of Police of Cincinnati, Ohio, gives us pause to consider whether we truly face the facts of human sexual foibles more honestly and frankly than our great-grandfathers did. More to the point, we might consider whether enforcement policies have progressed or fallen behind in practicality.

Cincinnati—1892. "The police of one city at least have fallen under condemnation, and it is but reasonable to suppose that our department may have to face a storm of censure in the same direction, and be forced into a position under the commands of the mayor, as in Pittsburgh, where the effort was a failure, to drive the notorious scarlet women out of the city as homeless, unhappy vagabonds. It is a well-known fact that the police recognize the criminal dangers that lurk around houses of ill-fame; but they further recognize that attempts to suppress them do not eradicate the evil, but serve only to disperse the women into rooms and dwelling-places in all quarters of the city, even the most reputable. The increased number of buildings in flats has markedly increased what the police know full well as 'roomers,' —prostitutes living in flats either entirely devoted to the purpose, partially so, or as places of assignation. It would raise a cry of indignation among the pious if there was established a French system of supervision, as if it was a municipal recognition of an immorality. The best municipal authorities have urged this supervision, which, although not absolutely certain to cure the evils, yet has, where honestly and conscientiously tried, mitigated the worst forms. A western city established a system of supervision that in the first year of trial reduced the annual average of new cases of venereal diseases, according to the statement of a prominent physician, fifty per cent. That system was gradually pro-

[14]William H. Masters and Virginia E. Johnson, *Human Sexual Response* (Boston: Little, Brown and Company, 1966).

Before Morality Had Decayed

ducing a marked change in the number of cases of moral adultery and fornication, when the religious element struck a blow and the system fell to pieces. It is a fact that, some years ago, when a member of the city's legislative body attempted to introduce an ordinance in the direction suggested, he was practically hounded out of political life. It is well worth while to caution any would-be critics that the State of Ohio does not recognize the Christian standard of adultery and fornication. The statute does not recognize that a single act of illicit intercourse is a crime, but that persons must 'cohabit,' that is, live together. The police have more than once arrested for single acts under circumstances most aggravating, but the legal definition of 'cohabit' has flung such cases out of court. The law recognizes the existence of prostitution, but it must be the act of a common prostitute; and then the fact that a person is such must be proven; merely so thinking does not lead to conviction. The law recognizes the existence of houses for prostitution, and has provided for the punishment of their keepers, their inmates, and the owners of the property; but not a single statute or ordinance affects the male visitor, unless some other offense should be committed, as, for instance, disorderly conduct, loitering, or some graver crime.

"Every conceivable plan has been adopted to prevent prostitution; the adulterer has been stoned, the prostitute made to wear a peculiar-colored garment, kept in walled quarters, imprisoned, publicly whipped, or deported wholesale, to colonies, and yet the woman still sits outside the door and proclaims that her good man has gone on a journey, and entices the unwary. The police are not agents of creeds and sects, but of the law, and must keep within the letter of the law as defined by the courts. If tomorrow an order should be issued by the mayor that every inmate should be convicted, the vice would not for a moment be stopped; for the instant the punishment imposed by law had been completed, that very moment those poor creatures on whom the law had laid its heavy hand would return, perchance not to old quarters, but would seek hiding-places less able to be controlled, and such crimes as blackmail and extortion would run rampant. The fault in prostitution lies in the fact that the male escapes. Theft, every crime known, still exist in spite of law, whether of church or state, and the anathemas of pulpit or press cannot eradicate forever one single class of vice, for vice is of the individual. I have been led to submit this view of prostitution because I anticipate that our department is likely to be assailed in the near future by some busy critic, who assaults an evil, but gives neither a remedy nor suggests a prevention." Philip Deitsch, Superintendent of Police.[15]

[15]Hale, *Police and Prison Cyclopaedia*, pp. 231–33.

Cities That Nobody Planned

When People Respected
the Police

New York—1653. "The Burgher-watch had become dissatisfied, as much with the nature of their duties as with the parsimony of their employers, and they went on a 'strike' in November, 1653. This excited the wrath of the choleric Director-General, who berated them roundly.... And it was all on account of the Burgher-watch not being supplied with firewood."[16]

Boston—1665. "Sir Robert Carr, sent over by the king to modify their abuses of the Colonial Government, spent his time on Sunday at a noted tavern called 'Noah's Ark,' in Ship Street. The governor issued a warrant against Sir Robert, for violation of the Sunday law, and Richard Bennet, the Constable, was sent to make the arrest. Sir Robert caned the officer and sent him away. The Governor then sent a summons for Sir Robert to appear before him, but he would not come. Arthur Mason, a spirited officer, was then sent to bring Carr, when some high words arose between the officer and Carr, and ere long poor Mason found himself in prison for attempting to obey his superior, and was eventually fined for an honest effort to do his duty, the Governor being glad to find a scapegoat in the person of his subordinate. ... Soon after this, cages were set up about town to put violators of the Sabbath in, and constables were ordered to 'search out and arrest Quakers.' "[17]

Boston—1709. "They [constables, watchmen] petition for leave to prosecute those who abuse them while on duty."[18]

Boston—1733. "At town meeting, an application was made to have Matthew Young appointed watchman, 'that he and his children do not become a town charge.' "[19]

Boston—1748. "Able-bodied watchmen allowed seven pounds, ten shillings per month, but fined twenty shillings for getting asleep on duty."[20]

[16]Augustine E. Costello, *Our Police Protectors: History of the New York Police* (New York: Police Pension Fund, 1885), p. 10.
[17]Savage, *Police Records and Recollections*, p. 17.
[18]*Ibid.*, p. 21.
[19]*Ibid.*, p. 26.
[20]*Ibid.*, p. 28.

Boston—1789. "Several burglaries having been committed, it was said, 'It is high time the watchmen were overhauled; they have been asleep since New Year's. The captains are generally men in their prime, aged from ninety to one hundred years, and the crew only average about fourscore [80], and so we have the advantage of their age and experience, *at least the robbers do*."[21]

Boston—1802. "The market-house robbed. The next day a newspaper paragraph said. 'It is remarkable that the broken door of the market-house is just forty feet from the watchhouse.' "[22]

Boston—1819. "A committee of the Selectmen made several visits to the watchhouses in the night time, and reported as follows: . . . '*January 12*. Another visit. Find too many watchmen doing duty inside. *January 20*. . . . South Watch doing good duty, but the two constables are asleep. . . . *February 3*. At one o'clock, visited South Watch: constable asleep. One and one-half o'clock, at Centre Watch, found constable and doorman asleep. Two o'clock, at North Watch found constable and doorman asleep, and a drunken man kicking at the door to get in.' The Inspector recommends *that the doorman be required to wake the constable when necessary*."[23]

Boston—1821. "Several burglaries having been committed, some persons were very severe on the Watch, and said 'They care for nothing but their pay, and are sure to get that; give us a private watch.' Others said, 'A private watch like the one in 1816, as soon as the stores are closed, would be found at the Exchange, sipping coffee. The only safe way is for merchants to watch themselves.' Others said, 'Who will work faithfully all night for the bare stipend of fifty cents.' "[24]

Chicago—1861. "A 'board of complaint,' consisting of the city marshal and the commanders . . . was created by Mayor Wentworth. This board met in the basement of the Court House, 'where all who had complaints to make were heard and answered.' . . . many important changes were made in the rules and regulations governing the force. The eccentricities of the mayor, his method of dealing with police officers, his interference in the most trivial details of police affairs, created very general discontent among the people."[25]

---

[21] *Ibid.*, p. 42
[22] *Ibid.*, p. 49.
[23] Savage, *Police Records and Recollections*, pp. 58–59.
[24] *Ibid.*, p. 60.
[25] Flinn, *History of the Chicago Police*, p. 96.

Cities That Nobody Planned

Chicago—1862. "One of the characters of the time was a certain 'Captain' Hyman, a professional blackleg and gambler, who was wont while in liquor to go about town intimidating people by whipping out a revolver and threatening death to anybody who crossed him in any way. One evening . . . Hyman took possession of the Tremont House office, and, revolver in hand, defied anybody to arrest him. The guests fled and the house police, as well as the officer on that beat, were afraid to go near him."[26]

One more glimpse into the lives, work, and status of policemen comes from historical accounts of efforts to regulate and discipline officers; such efforts were sometimes inspired by the behavior of policemen, sometimes by a less cordial regard for law enforcement officials.

New York—1674. Regulations: "That whosoever shall come upon ye Wattch, that is overcharged with drinke, hee or they shall pay halfe the aforementioned fine; but if abusive or Quite Drunke the whole fine to be paid as if absent and secured upon the Wattch all Night. . . .

"That whosoever shall presume to make any quarrell upon the wattch, upon the account of being different nations or any other pretense whatsoever, hee or they shall pay a whole fine and be liable to such further censure as the merit of the cause shall require."[27]

This reference to "different nations" may be interpreted as being the first indication of police department factionalism based upon nationalistic attitudes of immigrant policemen. It should be of particular interest to those who believe that ethnic and racial conflicts are unique in our generation.

New York—1684. "At a meeting of the Common Council held at the City Hall on October 13 . . . it was ordered that 'any persons chosen to serve in any of the offices following, and shall refuse to serve, shall pay the fine hereinafter expressed, viz:

A Constable	5 pounds.
An Assessor	3 pounds.
A Common Councilman . .	7 pounds, 10 shillings.
An Alderman	10 pounds.
The Mayor	20 pounds.

[26] Ibid., p. 104.
[27] Costello, Our Police Protectors, pp. 22–23.

When People Respected the Police

The fines to be paid to the Citty Treasurers for the publique use of the Citty.' "[28] (Recruitment problems apparently have been with the police occupation since its inception in North America.)

Boston—1825. "Watchmen found asleep, to be discharged."
             1843. "The Captain of the Watch fined for smoking in the street."
             1848. "Marshal Tukey fined for fast driving."[29]

Chicago—1870s. "On one occasion, . . . to go back a few years—three toughs set upon and beat a policeman in Captain O'Donnel's precinct. One of the fellows was captured a month or two after, and locked up. The captain was sitting in front of the station one night, when he heard groans from the cell-room. Rushing down stairs, he caught the officer who had been beaten cruelly abusing the prisoner. Seizing the blackguard in blue, the captain hurled him out of the cell, and against the opposite wall, nearly knocking him senseless. 'You coward!' he exclaimed; 'I've a notion to break your neck!' The officer begged his captain not to say anything about it, or to deny it. 'I'll not perjure myself for the whole police force, but I won't volunteer evidence, if not asked for.' He was asked, and told the story in court. But there is no more beating prisoners in cells at Twelfth Street."[30]

Concord, N.H.—1892. Report of the Chief. "A few years ago there existed in this city a strong prejudice against the police department, which at this time has not entirely disappeared. People who are constantly finding fault with the police are standing in their own light, for they are their servants and they would be supported.

"No police department that does its work fearlessly and well can hope for general favor. Every year hundreds of individuals are arrested and punished for violations of known laws, and it is not expected that they or their friends will call a mass meeting and pass resolutions commendatory to the department or any of its members."[31]

Denver—1892. Report of the Chief. "No taint of official corruption or prostitution of authority attaches to any member of the force. Brutal clubbing, severity, and unkind treatment of prisoners, which are frequently noticed in the newspapers of other cities, form no part of the record of the Denver police.

---

[28] *Ibid.,* p. 27.
[29] Savage, *Police Records and Recollections,* p. 87.
[30] Flinn, *History of the Chicago Police,* p. 359.
[31] Hale, *Police and Prison Cyclopaedia,* pp. 250–51.

Cities That Nobody Planned

"It cannot be expected that the police force can escape a certain amount of censure and criticism; and quite often harsh criticism, too, is made, when, if the truth had been fully known, commendation would have been bestowed. While performing the many duties required by the ordinances above referred to, the officer who does his duty is too often regarded by many as a common nuisance, and frequently meets with treatment which severely tries his patience."[32]

San Francisco—1892. Report of the Chief. "For a long time we were troubled with complaints from prisoners of losing property that was taken from them in the search when they were booked at the stations. After a good deal of trial I hit upon an expedient that prevented all such leakage. Whenever anything is taken from a prisoner now it is carefully described on the register sheet opposite his name by the officer in charge of the book."[33]

When Policemen Were Crimefighters

A fundamental adjustment which confronts every young policeman is the reality of his everyday work, contrasted with his pre-service notions about law enforcement, and often with recruitment descriptions of action-filled careers and "crime fighting." Patrolmen typically aspire to become detectives or department commanders, the former for fulfillment in their work, the latter for status. And in their adjustment to the more mundane service assignments they perform (some 80 percent of police work), policemen come to accept the folklore that at one time police work was largely crime fighting and that service functions have gradually been accepted, but only recently, as legitimate police responsibilities, to the neglect of the primary police mission. This bit of occupational belief deserves looking into, if only because it lends a nagging tinge of illegitimacy to the bulk of current police assignments, creating a rationale for unenthusiastic performance.

The following excerpts from accounts of law enforcement written in the nineteenth century provide a glimpse of policemen, their way of life, and their work, from the earliest

[32]*Ibid.*, pp. 256–57.
[33]*Ibid.*, p. 420.

colonial times in North America. The first five excerpts deal with conditions in the Dutch colony of New Amsterdam.

In 1624 Peter Minuit, the first Director-General (of the Dutch West India Company) arrived at New Netherland. His council . . . had supreme authority, and all its proceedings, whether criminal or civil, were instituted and conducted by an officer called a 'Schout Fiscal,' whose duties were equivalent to those performed by a sheriff and an attorney-general . . . enforcing and maintaining the placards, laws, ordinances . . . resolutions and military regulations of their High Mightinesses . . . protecting the rights, domains and jurisdiction of the Company, and executing their orders. . . . [he] superintended all prosecutions and suits . . . [could not] arraign, nor arrest any person on a criminal charge, except on information previously received, or unless he caught him [in the act] . . . and after trial he saw to the faithful execution of the sentence pronounced by the judges . . . attended to the commissaries arriving from the Company's outposts and to vessels arriving from or leaving for Holland, inspected their papers, and superintended the loading and discharging of their cargoes."[34]

1650s. "The Governor issued regulations for the better observance of the Sabbath; interdicting the tapping of beer during the hours of divine service or after ten o'clock at night; brawling and all kinds of offenses . . . [observing] that 'Almost one full fourth part of the City of New Amsterdam have become bawdy houses for the sale of ardent spirits, tobacco, and beer.' "[35]

[Enforcement functions included] "removal of hog-pens and out-houses from the highway; prohibiting trespass. . . ."[36]

December, 1655. "An ordinance interdicted the firing of guns and planting of May-poles, from which, as alleged, there had resulted much drunkenness, together with lamentable accidents. Beating of the drum, firing, pole-planting and the sale of liquor were interdicted under a penalty of twelve guilders for the first offence, twenty-four for the second, and arbitrary correction for the third offence. The fines so imposed were equally divided among the officer, the poor, and the prosecutor."[37]

In 1656. "A Watch, composed of a corporal's guards, was ordered to patrol the city on Sundays during divine service."[38]

[34]Costello, *Our Police Protectors*, pp. 3–4.
[35]*Ibid.*, pp. 5–7.
[36]*Ibid.*, p. 7.
[37]*Ibid.*, p. 10.
[38]*Ibid.*, p. 12.

Cities That Nobody Planned

New York—1702 "A new duty was imposed on the Constables of the several wards. This was to visit every house, and see whether the inhabitants kept the number of fire buckets required by law. . . . The Constables were required to 'make a presentment of all such persons as shall neglect or refuse to clean their streets, and of all such as in any way break the Holy Sabbath, or commit other misdemeanors.' "[39]

Philadelphia—1811. "There are fourteen constables, one for each ward; and until the present year, one high constable, who is required to walk the streets daily with his mace in his hand, and examine all vagrants and disorderly persons, and upon refusal to give him an account of their residence and employment, or not giving a satisfactory account, to carry such persons before the mayor or an alderman to be dealt with according to law. . . ."[40]

Chicago—1860s. "To be a policeman in those days was no sinecure. Patrol wagons were unknown, and the police were accustomed to impress into the service any description of vehicle which might be at hand to transport drunken and unruly men to the lock-up . . . Lieutenant Beadell . . . tells a story of how, for the want of some better conveyance, he loaded drunken Jimmy Kilfoil, a notorious Archer Avenue bum, into a wheelbarrow and pushed him from the vicinity of the old steam quarry to the Archer Avenue station, a distance of two miles."[41]

Chicago—1865. "Some of the earliest experiences to develop the sturdy personal courage of the men, occurred in the spring of 1865, when the police were largely employed in corralling soldiers and returning them to their regiments. But this work was discounted by the period after the war, before Grant ordered that no liquor should be sold to discharged soldiers on their way home. The returning heroes several times seemed about to take possession of the city, and few of the police officers of that day escaped numerous beatings at the hands of the disbanded bluecoats, while the latter were spending their battle-earned money on bad whiskey."[42]

Chicago—1869. ". . . the Twelfth Street district . . . was covered by only seventeen men, and no patrol wagons. The men had to

[39]*Ibid.*, p. 31.

[40]James Mease, "Municipal Services," in *The American City: A Documentary History*, ed. Charles N. Glaab, (Homewood, Ill.: Dorsey Press, 1963), p. 33.

[41]Flinn, *History of the Chicago Police*, p. 106.

[42]*Ibid.*, p. 355.

When Policemen Were Crimefighters

carry helpless 'drunks' on their shoulders to the station then."[43]

Chicago—1877. "It was during the street-car troubles. A car had been taken from the men in charge of it, including an officer, when Officers Lewis and Ptassec, two of the smallest men in the second precinct came along. They charged the mob, captured the car and set it running, and then chased the ringleader in the riot. . . ."[44]

Chicago—1870s. "The first beating Hubbard ever got was in protecting a woman named Murphy, who lived on Emerald street, . . . from her brutal husband. He had pulled the fellow off, and was struggling on the floor with him, when the wife deliberately locked the door, put the key in her pocket, and then, seizing a heavy stove-lifter, began beating the officer over the head. The arrival of the man on the next beat . . . alone saved Hubbard's life."[45]

Hoboken, N.J.—1892. "The Truant Officer's duty is to suppress truance, investigate complaints against the pupils of our public schools, to recover the public property that may be taken away by delinquent scholars.

"His [the officer detailed on the docks and wharves] duties are to attend all outgoing and incoming ships that land at our shore, no matter at what hour they come or go, so as proper order may be maintained on the docks and the passengers properly protected. He also assists the Overseer of the Poor in investigating the character of the applicants for poor relief."[46]

Los Angeles—1892. "My officers report to me that there are now but seven places in Chinatown in which fan-tan is ever played, and I think this is a smaller number than in any year since China-town has contained one hundred inhabitants. None of these games are run openly, or regularly, but only occasionally, when the wily players think the officers cannot get at them, and none of them are visited by other than Chinese players. To be perfectly frank in regard to this matter, I will say that I believe that there has always been more or less fan-tan playing in Chinatown, and that I believe there will be, unless sufficient officers are stationed there to keep at all times all of the Chinamen in sight, which would be rather an expensive undertaking. . . .

". . . the selling of Chinese lottery tickets has increased. The

[43]*Ibid.*, p. 357.
[44]*Ibid.*, pp. 361–62.
[45]*Ibid.*, p. 353.
[46]Hale, *Police and Prison Cyclopaedia*, pp. 289–90.

Cities That Nobody Planned

evidence necessary to make a conviction in these cases, under the present law, is almost impossible to secure. We have in the year made forty-two arrests, but have succeeded in making only thirteen convictions."[47]

Buffalo, N.Y.—1892. "There were 143,540 reports from officers ... total arrests, 21,383."[48]

Carbondale, Pa.—1892. "Total arrests, 183: 181 for drunk and disorderly; 2 for robbery."[49]

Everett, Mass.—1892. "Eight apothecaries were licensed, 6th class, $1.00 each."[50] (Licensing was done by the police department.)

LaCrosse, Wis.—1892. "... dog tax collected, $1,521.00. ... number of tramps lodged and fed at Station No. 2, 673, at a cost to the city of $47.25. ..."[51]

Lawrence, Mass.—1892. "The duty of enforcing the law in relation to the keeping and sale of intoxicating liquors is a difficult one."[52]

New Orleans, La.—1892. Among the listed functions of this police department were the following mandatory duties: "... guard the public health ... advise and protect immigrants, strangers, and travelers in public streets, at steamboat and ship landings, and at railroad stations. ..."[53]

New York City—1892. "Nine thousand, three hundred and twenty-seven licenses issued from January 1 to December 31, 1892. ... $1,523,780 received for licenses."[54]

Omaha, Nebr.—1892. "Experience leads me to believe that a police officer patrolling his beat, with a long wooden club in his hand or belt, is not calculated to produce the effect in the minds of criminals or citizens generally that he would if the club were out of sight. I have, therefore, caused the clubs not to be worn

[47]*Ibid.*, pp. 307–8.
[48]*Ibid.*, p. 215.
[49]*Ibid.*, p. 219.
[50]*Ibid.*, p. 268.
[51]*Ibid.*, p. 298.
[52]*Ibid.*, p. 301.
[53]*Ibid.*, p. 339.
[54]Hale, *Police and Prison Cyclopaedia*, p. 347.

When Policemen Were Crimefighters

except by police officers doing night duty during the winter months."[55]

St. Louis, Mo.—1892. "Number of lodgers given shelter in police station in 1892, 11,784."[56]

Arrests for drunkenness and alcohol-related misdemeanors seem to have changed very little since 1892. A sampling of Hale's survey statistics shows that from 38 to 99 percent of all arrests were made for drunkenness and drunk and disorderly conduct. Austin, Texas, was at the low end and Carbondale, Pa., at the high end of the spectrum. The Chief of Police of Atlantic City, N.J., where 81 percent of all arrests were for drunkenness, reported that "Most of the drunken people that are arrested come here drunk from other cities."[57]

When the Country Stood Together

Major disorders in our cities create emotional stresses which make it difficult for us to have any clear understanding of these events. Perhaps it is not any single riot or the large-scale consequences of any one riot which are so disturbing, but rather the chain reaction of multiple riots—the impression of a long-fused string of explosive charges planted across the nation, detonating in succession. Whatever the emotional disturbance may arise from, a result of it is a tendency to regard current riots as destroyers of the entire social system. In short, their destructive potential is exaggerated, and the capacity of the social system to repair itself and survive is underestimated.

From colonial days to the present, Americans have engaged in violent behavior—rioted—over a great variety of issues. At times these issues have been patriotic, religious, economic, ethnic or racial, ideological, and occupational. Some of the incidents started in good fun between groups supporting quaint beliefs; others have been serious, some grotesque. But it is interesting to note that no major disorder

[55]*Ibid.*, p. 356.
[56]*Ibid.*, p. 389.
[57]*Ibid.*, p. 196

Cities That Nobody Planned

resulted from a single, one-time, immediate cause. All of the riots studied were found to have several layers of tension behind them: some of the tensions were generations old, and others had grown over a few years. Also there were the more recent and shorter-duration tensions of a specific period ("long hot summers," the period of a labor strike, a political campaign), and finally, the hot surge of tension caused by a precipitating incident. Observers of past times have generally recorded at least two and often three layers of issues underlying riots. A list of disorders which have punctuated the growth of the United States and then a few summarized descriptions of completely diverse kinds of riots follows. They are of interest primarily because they occurred at a distance in time sufficiently remote to make possible an understanding of them unclouded by current issues and passions.

Major American Disorders

1765 Stamp Act Riots in Boston and New York
1771 The Regulators
1772 Burning of the *Gaspee*
1774 Resistance to the Boston Port Bill
1784 Revolt against North Carolina
1786 Shay's Rebellion
1788 Doctors' Riot, or Anti-Dissection Riot
1794 Whiskey Rebellion in Pennsylvania
1795 Demonstrations against the Jay Treaty
1798 Virginia and Kentucky Resolutions
1799 Fries Rebellion
1832 Tariff Nullification
1842 Dorr Rebellion
1844 Anti-Catholic Riots in Philadelphia
1849 Astor Place Riot in New York City—31 killed, 150 wounded, 86 arrested
1851 San Francisco Committee of Vigilance
1854 Struggle in Kansas over slavery
1855 German Tavern-Keepers' Revolt in Chicago; many killed, hundreds wounded by gunfire
1863 Conscription Riots in Boston and New York City, many killed, hundreds injured
1871 Anti-Chinese Riot in Los Angeles; 23 Chinese killed (18 in one afternoon)
1871 Orange Riots in New York City; 33 killed, 91 wounded

1877 Great labor strikes in West Virginia, and Pittsburgh, Pennsylvania; in 2 days, 16 soldiers and 50 strikers killed; 125 locomotives, 2,000 freight cars and a depot burned and destroyed; many killed and wounded in Chicago

1913 Ludlow Massacre; more than 50 killed

1919 Chicago Race Riot; 38 killed, 537 injured

1921 Tulsa Race Riot; 30 killed, several hundred injured

1943 Detroit Race Riot; 34 killed, 700 injured

1964 Race riots in New York City, Rochester, Philadelphia, Jersey City, Paterson, Elizabeth, and Chicago; 6 killed, 952 injured

1965 Los Angeles (Watts) Race Riot; 36 killed, 895 injured.

Boston—1765

INCIDENT:	Stamp Act Riots[58]
YEAR:	1765
LOCATION:	Boston (Concurrent locations: other colonies; less destructive riots)
PROTAGONISTS:	British government vs. Sons of Liberty.
GENERATIONAL ISSUES:	Presence of British troops in the colonies; oppressiveness of colonial government.
TRANSIENT ISSUES:	Sons of Liberty movement; tactless commands of the government.
PRECIPITANT:	Appointment of Stamp Distributor; organized agitation by the Sons of Liberty; a hanging in effigy from the "Liberty Tree."
POLICE INVOLVEMENT:	Chief Justice and Sheriff of Suffolk County were stoned when they attempted to persuade a mob to disperse. The mob destroyed the home of the newly appointed Stamp Distributor. On another day a law officer read the

[58]Willard A. Heaps, *Riots, U.S.A., 1765–1965* (New York: The Seabury Press, Inc., 1966), pp. 9–18.

Cities That Nobody Planned

riot act to a mob forming under the Liberty Tree. This mob left to destroy the office of the Vice Admiralty Court, where they burned all records, and also the new home of the Comptroller of Customs; here they "enjoyed the contents of his wine cellar."[59] Later that day the mob completely demolished the mansion of the Chief Justice. He had opposed the Stamp Act but as noted above, had previously sought to dissuade the mob from violence. At least 11 violent disorders occurred in this general pattern.

DISPOSITION: The Stamp Act was never enforced; it was repealed in 1766. Six or seven arrestees were released by the rioters, "who had forced the jailer to give up the keys."[60]

New York—1788
INCIDENT: Doctors' Riot,[61] or Anti-Dissection Riot
YEAR: 1788
LOCATION: New York City
PROTAGONISTS: Medical students and faculty of the New York Hospital vs. neighborhood workmen
GENERATIONAL ISSUES: No legitimate means of obtaining human bodies for medical studies. Growth of medical science, development of sci-

[59]*Ibid.*, p. 14.
[60]*Ibid.*, p. 16.
[61]*Ibid.*, pp. 19–29.

Major American Disorders

TRANSIENT ISSUES:

PRECIPITANT:

POLICE INVOLVEMENT:

entific method in medical education.

Medical students stole bodies, at first from the potter's field and Negro graves, later from a church graveyard. Newspapers criticized the activity, and public anger grew.

A curious boy, peeking into the dissection class, was chased off by a student who held up a human arm, telling the boy it was his mother's. By grisley coincidence, the boy's mother had recently died; her husband discovered that her grave had been opened and the body removed. He gathered a mob of more than 1,000 and demolished much of the medical school. Parts of human bodies were paraded by rioters to recruit a larger mob, which now included "sailors, loafers, criminals and motley mischief-makers."[62]

Sheriff, accompanied by the mayor, rescued four medical students in the initial incident. Lacking sufficient officers and unable to disperse a mob surrounding the hospital-medical school, the sheriff organized an 18-man military detachment and marched on the crowd. The mob mocked them and threw dirt and stones at them. The force withdrew and then returned,

[62] *Ibid.*, p. 22.

Cities That Nobody Planned

whereupon the mob smashed their muskets, chased off the troops, and stormed the jail, where the doctors had taken refuge. There followed ten additional confrontations of mobs (now numbering some 5,000) and military units. At least seven persons were killed and nine seriously injured. Most injuries were not recorded. The militia finally used armed force to quell the major disorder.

DISPOSITION: Grand Jury recommendations for penalizing doctors and students were dropped by the court. Hospital authorities dismissed from the staff those doctors and students who had been in the dissecting room when the precipitating incident occurred, and fined each offender $20. A law was enacted to supply a limited number of cadavers for medical education.

Philadelphia—1844
INCIDENT: Anti-Catholic Riots[63]
YEAR: 1844
LOCATION: Philadelphia (Concurrent locations: many other cities during the 1840s and under the Know-Nothing movement of the 1850s)
PROTAGONISTS: American Republicans (Nativists) vs. Irish Catholic immigrants
GENERATIONAL ISSUES: Religious intolerance based on belief "that the loyalty

[63]Heaps, *Riots, U.S.A.,* pp. 30–38.

	of Irish immigrants would be owed to Rome and the Pope rather than to their new country and that cheap Irish labor would lower American standard of living."[64]
TRANSIENT ISSUES:	Bishop asked school board to excuse Catholic children from reading King James version of the Bible so that they could be instructed in the Catholic translation. Nativists attacked this request (approved by the board) as a move to take the Bible out of the classroom.
PRECIPITANT:	Huge gathering of Nativists in the middle of the Irish section of the city. A fight started and moved into the street. Guns were fired from buildings into the crowd by Irish residents. Nativists fought back with bricks, one of them was killed and many wounded.
POLICE INVOLVEMENT:	First the militia, then the citizen police and a sheriff's posse intervened in the three major pitched battles between the Irish and Nativists. The mob fired cannon into the military force and sniped from upper-story windows and rooftops. Nativist rioters engaged military and police units in pitched battles. Twenty to twenty-four were killed, more than a hundred seriously injured. One arrest.

[64]*Ibid.*, pp. 30–38.

Cities That Nobody Planned

DISPOSITION:	Two grand jury hearings blamed the Catholics for the riot, citing their efforts "to exclude the Bible from our public schools."[65]

New York—1849

INCIDENT:	Astor Place Riot[66]
YEAR:	1849
LOCATION:	New York City
PROTAGONISTS:	Anti-British theatre patrons vs. English actor McReady and Astor Place Opera House
GENERATIONAL ISSUES:	Anti-British feeling generated over a long period by critical articles written about America by British travelers. Native American movement generated national hatreds.
TRANSIENT ISSUES:	National feelings focused on the prime British actor and the prime American actor of the time; each was treated rudely in the other's land. A downward spiral to violence occurred in the United States.
PRECIPITANT:	A McReady performance of *Macbeth* at the Astor Place Opera House was greeted with "Down with the English hog!" and then continual catcalling; a shower of pennies, fruit, and finally chairs. The following night McReady was persuaded by 48 leading citizens to appear again. Nativists circulated handbills citing a (fictitious) threat to McReady's detractors by British seamen then in port.

[65] *Ibid.*, p. 38.
[66] *Ibid.*, pp. 39–60.

Major American Disorders

POLICE INVOLVEMENT: Nativists attended the performance to disrupt it. Audience included 1,800 men and 6 women. Police removed the riotous 10 percent of the audience. Nativists rioted outside the theatre, where a great crowd had gathered through curiosity. Many windows were broken, and stones hit the audience. The outside mob was swelled by ruffians. Police and infantry fought the mob without gunfire for some time, but they sustained many serious injuries from paving blocks and bricks. Then a pistol shot from a rioter hit a troop commander; an unsuccessful bayonet charge was ordered, warning shots were fired, and finally, three volleys were fired into the mob. Despite many deaths and injuries, the mob continued the fight until two cannon were loaded with grapeshot and aimed; the rioters then dispersed. Thirty-one were killed, 150 seriously injured, and 86 arrested.

DISPOSITION: A Nativist resolution censured the police and military for their "barbarous treatment of peace-loving citizens." A coroner's jury found police and military action justified. Ten rioters were finally tried, found guilty, and sentenced to varying jail terms. "Before the Astor

Cities That Nobody Planned

Place Riot it was the legal opinion that no one could be prosecuted for a riot, as it was presumed to be 'the natural effect of political passion.' Judge Daly's charge completely reversed this concept, and prosecution for rioting became accepted under American law."[67]

Chicago—1855

INCIDENT:	German Tavern-Keepers' Revolt[68]
YEAR:	1855
LOCATION:	Chicago
PROTAGONISTS:	Native American, Know-Nothing political party vs. German immigrants and tavern-keepers of the North Side
GENERATIONAL ISSUES:	Election of Native American mayor and his commitment to suppress immigrants, and drive them out of business. Nativist reaction to great migrations from the British Isles and Germany during the 1830s and 1840s.
TRANSIENT ISSUES:	Nativist-inspired high liquor license fees, which would have driven out of business the hundreds of small beer dealers of Chicago, nearly all of whom were German immigrants.
PRECIPITANT:	The arrest of more than 200 German saloonkeepers for violation of a previously unenforced Sunday closing law. A test-case criminal trial was dis-

[67]*Ibid.*, p. 49.
[68]Flinn, *History of the Chicago Police*, pp. 72–79.

Major American Disorders

POLICE INVOLVEMENT: turbed by a demonstration of 500 Germans and a counterdemonstration at Clark and Randolph streets.

Captain Nichols, who headed the police department, cleared the streets and dispersed the mob upon orders from the mayor. A few men who resisted were arrested and taken into custody. That night, North Side Germans decided to cross the river and "rescue the prisoners. The rioters armed themselves with shotguns, rifles, pistols, clubs, knives, and every species of weapon...."[69] The spirit of revolt was heightened by rumors of a "raid" and by speeches exhorting immigrants to revolt against impending "slavery." "... the bridge opened, and the rioters swarmed across, only to be met by a solid body of policemen.... A collision was expected, and it came. Cries of 'Shoot the Police,' 'Pick out the stars,' rose from the mob, accompanied by the cracking of guns and pistols. The police replied without waiting for orders, and for several minutes there was a hot engagement in the vicinity of the Sherman House. A German, whose name is lost, levelled a double-barrelled shot gun at Officer Hunt

[69]*Ibid.*, pp. 75–77.

Cities That Nobody Planned

and blew off his left arm. Sheriff Andrews . . . ordered a young man named Frazer . . . to return the fire. He did so, shooting the German dead. A large number were wounded on both sides, and several mysterious funerals occurred on the North Side within the next few days. . . ."[70]

DISPOSITION: Sixty prisoners were added to those already being held, and the mayor ordered two military companies to protect the Court House with their artillery. But the riot was over, and "Nearly all the cases against the imprisoned rioters were dismissed. . . ."[71]

Boston—1863
INCIDENT: Conscription Riot[72]
YEAR: 1863
LOCATION: Boston (Concurrent location: New York City two days before)
PROTAGONISTS: Citizens opposed to lottery-type draft vs. Provost Marshal's serving draft notices in Boston.
TRANSIENT ISSUES: General opposition to the conscription, "as unconstitutional, unjust, and oppressive . . ."[73] especially the provision that a man was entitled to exemption if he paid a $300 fee or furnished a substitute.

---

[70] *Ibid.*, p. 78.
[71] *Ibid.*, p. 79.
[72] Savage, *Police Records and Recollections*, pp. 347–70.
[73] *Ibid.*, p. 349.

Major American Disorders

	Hourly newspaper specials on the New York conscription riot.
PRECIPITANT:	A woman attacked two marshals, whom she mistakenly thought had come to take her husband into the army. She was joined by neighbors, passersby, and finally the entire crowd watching the draft lottery became involved.
POLICE INVOLVEMENT:	Several policemen were attracted to the disorder and beaten by the crowd; more were sent in with the same results. The rioters then surrounded one of the police stations and were seen to be armed. That night several armed mobs moved about the city, largely beating strangers, police, and members of the military forces. There was window smashing and looting in the commercial districts, and several cases of arson occurred. At least eight were killed, many were seriously injured, and approximately a dozen persons were arrested.
DISPOSITON:	Then, as now, there were serious questions about the causes. The police historian reported: "Whether the Conscription Riot ... was the result of regular and extensive organization, reaching far beyond the limits of our own city or State, for the purpose of aiding the Rebellion, or whether it was only composed of a combination of

Cities That Nobody Planned

men limited within the bounds of Boston and the surburban towns, or whether it was only a spontaneous outbreak, which is at any time liable to happen in all thickly populated places, is a question not well understood."[74] No arrests or prosecutions are recorded.

Los Angeles—1871

INCIDENT:	Anti-Chinese Riot[75]
YEAR:	1871
LOCATION:	Los Angeles (Concurrent locations: San Francisco, 1877; Denver, 1880; Wyoming, 1885
PROTAGONISTS:	White residents vs. Chinese community
GENERATIONAL ISSUES:	A shortage of manpower in the mining and railroad industries inspired the importation of shiploads of indentured coolies. Even though profits increased for company owners, there was a reduction of wages for whites; racial prejudice followed.
TRANSIENT ISSUES:	To avoid payment of the bride-price, a young man from one tong [a Chinese family society or organization] married a girl owned by a rival tong in a civil ceremony. Tong warfare ensued among the Chinese of Los Angeles. There was some gunfire between the rival clans.
PRECIPITANT:	A policeman, one of the six-man Los Angeles force,

[74]*Ibid.*, pp. 368–69.
[75]Heaps, *Riots, U.S.A.*, pp. 61–71.

intervened in an intertong exchange of gunfire and was wounded. Soon after, a rancher assisting another policeman was fatally wounded. A large crowd (at least 10 percent of Los Angeles' population of 6,000) gathered at the false report that Chinese were "killing whites wholesale."

POLICE INVOLVEMENT: The marshal deputized guards, and surrounded the large building-courtyard in which most of the city's Chinese lived. A lynching occurred shortly afterward, and the mob shot 18 Chinese during the afternoon and hung their bodies in various places in the town. Others were hanged outright, many were mutilated. The police assisted in securing many Chinese in the jailhouse, even though some of the policemen were found to have participated in the shootings, and others were intimidated and prevented from interfering with lynching parties. Twenty-three Chinese are known to have been killed. $30,-000 was looted from Chinese quarters.

DISPOSITION: Arrests were variously reported at 30, 39, and 150. Ten men were brought to trial for the killing of a Chinese physician; eight were found guilty and given sentences of two to six years. A year later, the California Supreme Court

Cities That Nobody Planned

reversed the verdict, stating that the indictment charged only the killing of the Chinese, not murder.

New York—1871

INCIDENT:	Orange Riots[76]
YEAR:	1871
LOCATION:	New York City
PROTAGONISTS:	The Orange Societies vs. the "green" (Catholic) Irish
HISTORICAL ISSUES:	Two-hundred year quarrel between Orange-Protestant Irishmen and Catholic Irishmen, carried over from Ireland to New York.
TRANSIENT ISSUES:	Orangemen applied for a parade permit to celebrate an anniversary date of William of Orange, first Protestant monarch of Ireland. Permit at first refused on public safety grounds, later issued.
PRECIPITANT:	During the parade along a route lined by hostile Irish Catholics, a shot was fired from a window.
POLICE INVOLVEMENT:	Police in addition to a military regiment, were accompanying the Orangemen in large numbers. When the shot was fired from the window, without awaiting orders, the regiment fired into the crowd. Their first volley killed policemen as well as bystanders. Thirty-three were killed and 91 seriously injured.

[76]Costello, *Our Police Protectors*, pp. 244–48.

Major American Disorders

DISPOSITON: "Much indignation was
                               expressed at the action of
                               the troops for firing with-
                               out waiting for orders,
                               and firing so wildly as to
                               wound and kill some of
                               their own men."[77]

Some Comments on Serious Disorders

The following observations can be made from this brief examination of urban disorders and police-community tensions during the past two centuries.

1. Major disorders or riots have occurred frequently in the cities of the United States.
2. The causes of riots have been consistently identified as major social issues, for example, labor strikes; wartime conscription; social, racial, ethnic, religious, and nationalistic prejudice, and reactions to it.
3. Major disorders generated by social movements or by the reaction to government and all nonspecific "others" nearly always take the form of police-mob conflicts.
4. In disorders which involve two or more struggling factions, the police invariably become engaged as a third faction in an effort to restore tranquility. Their participation may assist or appear to assist the cause of one of the factions or, barring that, may invite the animosity of both factions, neither of which welcomes the attempt to end the contention.
5. Although riots and poor police-community relationships have both been frequently described in histories of the United States, the two phenomena have rarely been joined in a cause-effect relationship. Before the present decade, there was no mention of strained police-community relationships as a contributing factor to community disorders. On the other hand, there were several depictions of police commanders who, to their later benefit or detriment, established great riot suppression reputations during major disorders.
6. Following virtually every major disorder, according to

[77] Ibid., p. 246.

Cities That Nobody Planned

contemporary published accounts, the police have been criticized for (*a*) forebearance in the presence of public disruption and insults to the rule of law and (*b*) use of excessive force in dispersing mobs and restoring order. Additionally, the police have consistently been accused of (*a*) slowness in the deployment of force against riotous crowds or (*b*) a too quick, provocative use of force, which nourished the full-scale disorder.

7. Riots usually result in the arrest of many persons—with varying quality of identification and substantiation of charges. Disposition of the cases, however, has nearly always been discharge without prosecution, even when the number of deaths and serious injuries and the destructon of property have been great. This fact is seldom deplored in contemporary accounts of riots, even in those by police historians. It is as if there is tacit acknowledgement that grave social issues are being worked out.

Major American Disorders

A Society Nobody Intended

The Nature of Change

The causes of social change are not clearly understood even by those who specialize in the study of change. However, the effects and powerful impact of change are very well known to all of us. In the barbershop the increasing pace of change is replacing the weather as the choice conversational topic. And yet, to discuss change is not to understand it. Much like the weather the topic of change is infinitely discussable because of its infinite number of interpretations. We all have ideas about the causes and effects of change, and most of us casually add our observations to the mass conversation, but some observations are more accurate, better informed, and based upon broader perspectives than others. Although many of the casual comments about change appear to have a great deal of support in our common everyday experiences, contradictory observations do arise and often balk the conversation into a mute impasse or an ambiguous, no-win argument. This occurs most often when somebody fastens upon a single aspect of change as being primary, for instance: "Change is just a matter of cycles; if you study history, you see it happen over and over again and can understand and anticipate what is happening to us." This kind of statement is an invitation to a response like: "Technological innovations are at the heart of change, pushing us into new situations. There is no precedent for the pace and kind of change happening today." At some point in this kind of discussion, it is almost inevitable that one or more observers will attribute major change to "the boys in City Hall" or at the country club—the so-called community power structure—or to its polar opposites, "those outside agitators," the radicals.

chapter

4

✳ Thus, in the same brief conversation, it is not uncommon to hear that change is caused by the general nature of the world (cycles), by man's inventions (technology), and by small special-interest groups (power elites, radicals). All of this is interesting because it calls attention to the broad range of factors which seem to be associated with change. It suggests, also, that casual observations about change are not particularly useful—except possibly as time passers in the barbershop—to those who have some need to understand the nature of change.

Riding the Blade: the Cutting Edge of Change

Among all those who need some understanding of change, the policeman stands in the front row. He is at the cutting edge of social change, where all the tensions generated by a restless, milling society are expressed in human action. Holding an unspecified mandate to "keep order," the policeman discovers the very definitions of "order" changing as he proceeds through his career. Entering the police department as a recruit, he learns a set of ground rules and later finds that these rules no longer seem to apply. And yet, some aspects of the world seem never to change. It is not surprising, then, that so many law enforcement officers have expressed confusion and dismay at the rate and nature of change confronting them. In a very real sense, their roles as officers are undermined by great shifts in social values and direction; resistance to change is a logical response when personal obsolescence appears to be a result of that change. It is probable that one of the major aspects of police-community relations, at least for the individual police officer, is traceable to the problem of understanding the nature of change, and of reacting to change in a reasonable way.

Previously it was pointed out that most casual observations about change become fixed upon narrow aspects of it, and although these observations may be accurate and valid as far as they go, they are hopelessly incomplete as aids in gaining any real comprehension of social change. And policemen are vulnerable to this tendency toward simple explanations of complex events. Officers customarily deal with the

Riding the Blade: The Cutting Edge of Change

power of government; they wield it, and every day they use it. So it is not surprising to find that policemen often interpret social change as being a result of deliberate action by powerful groups—whether power elites, subversive radicals, or other special-interest groups. Interviews with law enforcement officers indicate a considerable belief on their part that most of what happens in a given community is a logical consequence of a planned strategy. Part of this orderly kind of perspective is probably caused by the policeman's mission and his training, which center upon the individual responsibility of each citizen. There is not much consideration in the criminal law or in public administration for large-scale, nonrational, unanticipated consequences resulting from the cumulative workings (interactions) of individual rational behavior. Both law and administration tend toward the establishment of authority and responsibility for initiating action and for outcomes. Thus, it is somewhat difficult for a police officer to accept as explanations of events that small-scale trends, errors, and reasonable actions accumulate into large-scale consequences intended by no one.

If social change is not simply a logical outcome of decisions made by powerful people, what accounts for it? Where does change originate, and what are its mechanical features? A very early model that attempted to explain social change consisted of the two variables found in Figure 1.

Fig. 1.

The implication is that as man increases his use of the environment, environment changes physically, man's view of it changes, and the environment as a factor enlarges the possibilities of technological innovation. For instance, man's discovering that coal burns and then following a surface vein of coal down into the ground by digging introduced an alternative to wood as fuel, and simultaneously the technological concept of taking useful things out of the earth by digging. This seemingly elementary fact takes on tremendous significance when you learn that many tribal civilizations never developed their technology to the point of digging below the earth's surface for useful materials. Thus their perception of environment

A Society Nobody Intended

was limited to naturally occurring surface features and forms of life. Consider, for a moment, how differently an American Indian hunter and a European industrialist must have viewed the ridges of Pennsylvania in 1850 or the St. Lawrence River, or in modern times the uranium-bearing ores of the western United States. Technological innovations redefine the environment—give it new and expanded meanings—while each new yield of the environment expands the possibilities for technological innovation and growth. Thus technology and habitat form a mutually expanding system, each contributing to the heightened possibilities of the other.

The early model, depicted in Figure 1 however, could be applied only to the most primitive of emerging social groups, those that had not yet developed even simple economic systems. For it becomes immediately apparent that other influences act upon technology and uses of the environment, and that social change is not simply a result of inventions and wider uses of the environment. Figure 2 adds the economic dimension to the more primitive scheme originally shown.

Fig. 2.

The implication of Figure 2 is that the interplay between technology and the environment produces an economy—a structure or system for handling the output of the environment—an economy that is ever increasing because of growing technology.

But the meaning of Figure 2 goes much further than that. Once the economic system has evolved from a primitive bartering structure to one involving money and other symbolic transfers of value, a fundamentally important change in the whole social format takes place, and the rate of social change jumps ahead. A money economy makes possible the accumulation of wealth—not feasible in primitive systems bartering perishable, bulky, and limited staples—and a sudden new capacity for large-scale enterprise. Thus, the interaction of technology and environment produced the need for an eco-

Riding the Blade: The Cutting Edge of Change

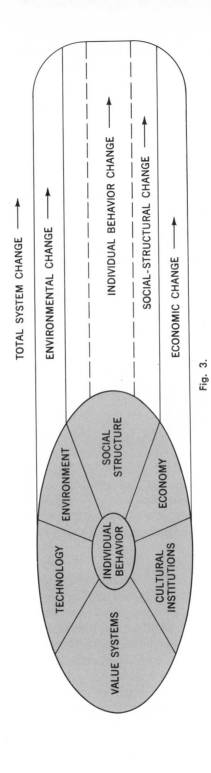

Fig. 3.

nomic structure, which, when it had evolved, vastly increased the means available for technological growth through a greater exploitation of natural resources, through experimentation, and through a systematic and scientific searching for new materials and new uses for them. The days of the purely accidental discovery of new environmental goodies, for example, coal, copper, and iron, were over. Our folklore abounds with cases of blundering enrichment among pioneering settlers, but the large-scale exploitation of oil deposits, uranium ores, and other environmental resources could not have occurred before the days of accumulated wealth, before the money economy.

And still, this model seems to be incomplete, unless we are willing to assume that all of the change going on about us results from scientific-industrial-economic expansion, certainly a narrow-gauge explanation for broad-gauge phenomena. Completely left out of the model are (1) *cultural values*—morals, ethics, interests, preferences—which are involved in so much of human behavior and which seem to change along with other parts of our world; (2) *the structure of our social system*, which contains privileged and less privileged positions, high status and low, wealth and poverty, professional and laborer, and other uneven distributions of valued things; and (3) *cultural institutions* such as schools, churches, criminal justice systems, governmental agencies, labor unions, and other organized ways of getting things done. These aspects of human society also change, and seem related to changes which occur in the environment, technology, and the economy.

A more complete model of change—one which seems to explain much more of what is happening in our world—thus includes the factors of technology, environment, economy, values, social structure, and cultural institutions. These factors operate within the behavior of individuals and groups and add up to enormous cumulative forces in major groupings of human beings. Figure 3 illustrates this point.

Some of the interactions of these variables as they influence the behavior of individuals and accumulate into larger social forces may be illustrated in the area of birth control.

1. The introduction and widespread use of a scientific innovation such as the birth control pill might be slower, more difficult, or impossible in a nation where the dominant religious beliefs forbid artificial contraception. This relationship might be expressed as in Figure 4.

Riding the Blade: The Cutting Edge of Change

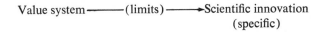

Value system ———— (limits) ————→ Scientific innovation
(specific)

Fig. 4.

A result of this relationship might be continued over-population. In a nation whose unemployment is already high, a secondary result would be increasingly depressed economy (Figure 5) and, perhaps, an unstable or repressive government.

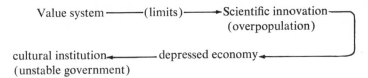

Value system ———— (limits) ————→ Scientific innovation
(overpopulation)

cultural institution ◄———— depressed economy ◄————
(unstable government)

Fig. 5.

2. Conversely, the birth control pill might be readily introduced in a country which had no dominant religious, moral, or other values opposed to contraception. Widespread contraception might lead to more leisure time for women, and thus a general movement toward employment of women outside the home. The greater incidence of working mothers of small families might in turn lead to less supervision in the home and greater numbers of children becoming delinquent or mentally ill. This highly speculative chain of relationships is represented in Figure 6.

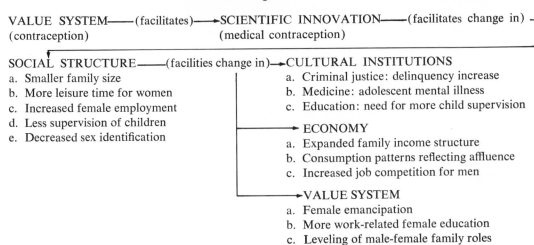

VALUE SYSTEM ———— (facilitates) ————→ SCIENTIFIC INNOVATION ———— (facilitates change in)
(contraception)   (medical contraception)

SOCIAL STRUCTURE ———— (facilities change in) ——→ CULTURAL INSTITUTIONS
a. Smaller family size
b. More leisure time for women
c. Increased female employment
d. Less supervision of children
e. Decreased sex identification

a. Criminal justice: delinquency increase
b. Medicine: adolescent mental illness
c. Education: need for more child supervision

→ ECONOMY
a. Expanded family income structure
b. Consumption patterns reflecting affluence
c. Increased job competition for men

→ VALUE SYSTEM
a. Female emancipation
b. More work-related female education
c. Leveling of male-female family roles

Fig. 6.

A Society Nobody Intended

If, as we are claiming, the process of change works out through a number of factors operating within the behavior of individuals and human groups of all kinds and descriptions and adds up to large-scale change, then it should be possible to trace to these factors some of the changes which have occurred in law enforcement in recent times. The following section deals with some relatively new conditions confronting police departments, which are attributable to changes in *environment, technology, the economy, social structure, value systems,* or *cultural institutions.* In some cases the reader may consider the situations as being caused by a factor other than that given here; the on-going, restless interaction of these factors often permits the tracing of long strings of relationships, none of which can truly be considered a beginning of the whole process.

The Factors of Change

Environment

Housing Projects. Particularly the high-rise variety, for the urban poor are considered by many police departments to be focal points of all our urban ills. These relatively new environmental features of many American cities are not the results of scientific innovation but rather of a curious interplay of our *social structures,* the *economy,* and governmental (*institutional*) application of certain political (social) *values* regarding poverty and land use. In any case, these high-density living units, concentrating into one area so many of a city's people who have not "made it," even marginally, often present environmental land mines to the police. Whether from hopelessness or boredom, residents of these architectural monstrosities engage—more so than others in the city population—in activities which are irritating, injurious, or even lethal to their project neighbors (most slum crime victimizes slum dwellers), to the unwary who blunder in, or to those who enter to provide services. With their miles of labyrinth-like corridors, their broken-lighted stairwells, and their robbery-encouraging elevators, high-rise housing projects constitute an almost unprotectable environment. Perhaps the only protection for those living here is to have nothing and be nothing

The Factors of Change

of value to others. In response to new community-security problems created by housing projects, the police have been able to do little more than take reports of the numerous crimes which occur and to investigate the more serious of them.

Interstate highways and expressways which cut through formerly cohesive neighborhoods of our cities have disrupted accustomed patterns of intracity movement, irritated those owning homes adjacent to them, produced noise and air pollution, created a new potential for high-speed traffic fatalities, and required that the local police adjust to the new use of that strip of city ground. Part of the adjustment consists of new traffic enforcement demands, and often education of the driving public to high-speed entry and exit tactics. The expressways also become part of the changed crime environment by providing for the criminal rapid movement between his residence and his crime target and a flexible exit route as well.

Population shifts to and within the city are of a more cyclic, on-going nature. The urban environment, considered both in the sense of streets and buildings and—in the sense of neighborhoods in transition as a group of habitats for shifting populations—requires of the police a continuing adjustment of territorial manpower deployment as well as constant attention to changes of rate and types of crime. Perhaps *ecology*, rather than *environment*, better expresses the total relationship of an urban territory and its inhabitants —that peculiar set of meanings given to a locale by those who live there and by those who view the scene from a specialized perspective, such as the police.

Technological Innovation

Consider the consequences of introducing into police work the patrol car and the two-way radio. The automobile increased the mobility of the officer, in the limited sense of movement between points in a large territory. The radio (and widely used telephone) cut the response time of requests for service from citizens, in the limited sense of providing a full-time communication linkage between the police station and the officer. But, as usual, these desirable, expected results of

A Society Nobody Intended

scientific innovation were accompanied by unanticipated side-effects.

One commonly recognized side effect of motorized patrol was the insulation of the police officer from the people of his patrol territory. How this physical isolation contributed to worsening police-citizen relationships has been analyzed in many publications. Largely unconsidered, however, was the effect of motorization upon the *crime prevention* techniques of the police. A prominant part of every police training effort, whether a formal academy program or an on-the-job apprenticeship, has long been the teaching of "suspicion arousers" or the development of alertness to incongruous actions or circumstances. Young officers have been trained to watch for cars parked with motors running, youngsters in expensive cars, persons loitering between buildings, fresh damage to automobiles, ladders in alleys, and innumerable other conditions worthy of examination. They have been taught to constantly observe; to question the normalcy, logic, and appropriateness of what they see and hear; to consider the "fit" of person, environment, and action.

Compare for a moment the situation of a lone patrolman walking a beat he knows well, who observes a person walking in an alley between two retail stores at 3:00 A.M. and that of an officer driving a patrol car, who sees a person driving an automobile in the warehouse district at 3:00 A.M. In the former case, the skillful officer would contrive to encounter the "suspicious" person at a place and under conditions favorable to himself, and unsettling to the other. Under these circumstances it is unnecessary for the officer to explicitly *initiate* the encounter (today called a field interrogation or interview); he merely lets it happen, perhaps with an ordinary greeting. And once confronted by the officer under incongruous conditions, the "suspected" person is under a conventional social obligation to acknowledge the policeman's presence and, especially if under tension, to account for his own presence. The ordinary give-and-take of personal encounters in everyday life provides a basis for this procedure, and unconventional responses to a confrontation with a policeman would be distinctive under these conditions.

Now, in the case of the motorized officer, consider the process of checking out the occupants of the vehicle which has aroused suspicion. First of all, there is no socially conventional way of getting at these occupants. To even see them clearly, the officer must explicitly initiate the encounter by signaling the car to stop. The mechanics of this process gives the vehicle's occupants time to organize their thoughts, and if a criminal intention is present, to conceal evidence, arm themselves, and otherwise counter the coming confrontation. What is important about all this is that the gestures which convey the intentions of the officer commit him to far more than the simple greeting of a pedestrian by an officer on the beat. In vehicle stops the officer telegraphs his action, increases the opportunity for violence and counteraction by persons disposed to it, and, in the eyes of most citizens, initiates a larger-scale encounter than the pedestrian stop. The officer is then faced with conducting this escalated operation whenever he perceives circumstances inappropriate enough, under the traditional definitions of police work, to require further investigation. In so doing, he must be concerned about overreacting and misreading gestures or incipient actions of the subjects on the one hand and "playing it cheap," to his own hazard on the other hand.

The Economy

The police personnel condition, in the view of most police administrators, has been significantly affected by cyclic upswings and downswings of the nation's economy. It is commonplace to observe that the police service gained a windfall of excellent manpower during the years of the Great Depression. Conversely, as high-status, lucrative occupations have become increasingly available in times of prosperity, police work has become less attractive and, consequently, has been less competitive for prime manpower.

Crime rates apparently relate to economic cycles also. But contrary to common-sense expectations, crime appears to increase in good times and recede during depressions. There may be several contributing factors to this effect. One may be, as Runciman[1] has pointed out, that those who have little become conservative and attempt to conserve what they have rather than seek after more. There is, in a word, less

---

[1] W. G. Runciman, *Relative Deprivation and Social Justice* (London: Routledge & Kegan Paul, Ltd., 1966), p. 6.

A Society Nobody Intended

risk taking when survival rather than unlimited gains, is the game. A second contributing factor may be that there are fewer available conspicuous targets of crime and less carelessness with property because of a heightened sense of vulnerability.

Value Systems

Sexual morality, for instance, at one time was considered very much the business of the state, as shown by the numerous statutes regulating the sexual conduct of consenting adults even in private and often prohibiting an enlightening assortment of sexual acts between man and wife. In some periods of our history it has been the custom to seek a unity between law and morality, and this tendency has had the support of a sizable number of religious denominations. However, it is probably inevitable in a pluralistic society such as ours that the many interpreters of morality eventually find the criminal law a cumbersome way of dealing with moral issues. Thus, major religious bodies currently advocate repeal of those criminal statutes which have been so ineffective in their self-defined roles as protectors of private and public morality. The current dominant view of clergymen is that criminal law should continue to protect all persons from victimization and public nuisances should be curtailed but that individual morality should be a function of conscience —a concern of the family and church, not of the government. The implications of this gradual shift of view by our churches and other cultural institutions (schools, legal institutions) are enormous for the police, whose charge of maintaining public order has been so generously defined over the years. It is simple enough for legal scholars and ecclesiastics to convene and derive new, pragmatic positions on matters such as private morality and the criminal law. It is quite another matter for a highly diffused body of some 400,000 police officers— who operate quite independently and are cohesive only in the sense of a shared occupation and certain traditions—to suddenly abandon the instrumentalized expressions of previous perspectives on law and morality. It s extremely difficult for them to give up habitual policies, procedures, and techniques for dealing with sexual activity occurring outside a very nar-

Value Systems

row set of limits. As anthropologists so often find, kinds of activity which once served a group need often continue in a mechanistic way long after a group need no longer exists; that is, structures outlive their usefulness.

Social Structure

One of the notable features of our social structure is its relationship with the educational system. In most modern societies there has been a direct connection between social class and educational attainment, in a mutually supportive system. That is, birth into a higher social class provides greater access to educational opportunity, and higher educational attainment leads to improved social and economic functioning, and thereby maintenance of social position. This pattern has been subtly different in the United States, where popular education, and especially the state university system, has enabled millions of young people to exceed the educational levels of their parents. This pattern has led to upward social mobility for many who would have been locked into their social status of birth in other societies.

Much of this American educational system has grown in response to the powerful cultural value placed upon aspiration and achievement—the pronounced theme of mobility and success. However, there are practical limits in the numbers of university-educated persons required to sustain the system, even in a society whose needs for professional services are very large. A recent educational development which addresses both the American aspiration pattern and the emerging need for greater numbers of sub-professionals is the community college or junior college system. It has been estimated that graduates of two-year college programs, who are being educated to fill occupational positions between the skilled trades and professionals, will become the most numerous educational category within a generation. This means that we will have created a new layer or social status within our social structure, all within a very short time.

If this educational group does become a majority of our population, it will be most interesting to discover whether it also becomes a political force and a dominant carrier of social values, as the working and middle classes have been in past

A Society Nobody Intended

times. The significance of this emerging educational pattern for the police can only be speculated upon. Certainly it raises the priority of higher education for law enforcement personnel. In 1940 only 39 percent of the American public had graduated from high school or college; in 1950 this had increased to 50 percent, and to 62 percent by 1960. Merely to remain average in this changing social structure, the police will need to greatly extend their level of educational attainment. Of additional significance is the nature of the clientele to be served by the police in future years. The sophistication and social awareness which grow with education will undoubtedly produce a more knowledgeable, demanding, and critical public. Considering the relationship between education and the status of occupations in the social structure, there can be no more critical matter on the agenda of law enforcement professionalizers than raising educational standards.

Cultural Institutions

As interacting agents of social change, cultural institutions are of particular interest because of their seemingly contradictory characteristics. Institutions are generally systems crystallized from persistent values, expressed as ways of getting things done. That is, through a history of trial and error, the valued processes of a society are boiled down to a few alternative "best ways" of doing the job. Passing useful information along to the next generation has taken the forms of folklore, father-son crafts, guilds, "mysteries," rituals, informal teaching, and highly organized specialized education. Maintaining order has ranged from a general involvement of all the adults in primitive cultures to bureaucratized structures in highly developed societies. Moral and spiritual beliefs have become instrumentalized as structures which carry on the beliefs and provide a means of producing everyday activity based upon the beliefs. Through some kind of institution, morality then becomes a basis for action.

Although our institutions are crystallizations of values and of the needs of society to maintain itself, these same institutions are at the *cutting edge* of change, in that they occupy a sharp point at which our ideals, beliefs, hopes, traditions, assumptions about the world, morals, ethics, and social organization rub very hard against the real world of living and action. Thus, even though institutions represent the tendency of our value systems and social structure to maintain themselves in a fairly stable form (a process sometimes called "The Establishment" by those who believe a dozen men in some back room control all of this), these institutions confront head-on all of the pressures for change. They include the legislative, administrative, and judicial branches of government; the schools, churches, social organizations, and "helping" professions (medical, welfare, rehabilitative); commercial-industrial enterprises; and communications media.

Law enforcement is part of one of these cultural institutions: the system of criminal justice. The criminal justice system in turn is loosely associated with other quite different institutions, which have as their primary or secondary objectives the *maintenance of social control.*

Transactions made by those in police uniform occur between *roles*, not between human beings, although the human carriers of the roles do not escape the consequences of the action. This is merely a very strong and quite strange way of making the point that while on duty a policeman is rarely able to function as a person. His identity as an officer easily overwhelms his personal characteristics and his identity as an individual human being. This phenomenon has been called stereotyping, prejudice, stigmatization, and also a form of social efficiency demanded in everyday life. There is, of course, a vital difference between an efficient designation of the police role as it relates to function and a stereotyped inference of unpleasant characteristics. The first is a form of social shorthand which gives us useful concepts such as "waiter," "scientist," "child," and "mother"; the latter, which would have us believe in uniformity within huge populations of human beings, gives us "kike" and "nigger," "flatfood," "fuzz," and "pig." Citizen perception of the police role ranges from the generally useful connotations through prejudiced interpretations. Sometimes these perceptions result from personal experiences with the police, but often they are related more directly to the citizen's own role in the community, and especially his membership in one of the several *subcultures* which make up our large, pluralistic social system. By "subculture" we refer to a part of the population which subscribes to the broad outlines of our way of life but whose concepts, beliefs, habits, art, apparel, dwellings, institutions, or implements differ markedly from what is customarily found in the majority population. A subculture also has the characteristic of persistence: it continues through time by renewing its membership in each generation, in effect, by reproducing itself.

Subcultures and Law Enforcement

X In pluralistic societies subcultures have always presented an interesting challenge to the forces of social control. In a large community if there is a dominant or conventional set of values, customs, and artifacts which closely determine how its members look and behave and which establish the limits of appropriateness, then a smaller group within the community which differs markedly in custom, dress, or behavior immediately demands a decision of the larger group. The decision is *whether social control will be predicated rigidly upon the dominant cultural norms or upon some other abstract standard.* This dilemma inherent in our open society has consumed much time, thought, and energy, and has been at the center of the law-morality relationship controversy for several generations.

Because it is not the kind of issue which can be decided precisely and equitably, working it out continues while we go on living and working and making difficult judgments about human conduct with the guidelines which have thus far flowed out of this continuous process.

Confronted with the need for performing his duties routinely, the police officer occupies the cutting edge of both social *change* and social *difference*. He works in all neighborhoods including those which do not resemble conventional ones, and when changing values, customs, or ways of behaving antagonize the more conventionally oriented residents of the community, the policeman is called. But, for some reason, even social change appears easier to accept than the unconventionality of subcultures within the community. The policeman is often called upon to mediate disputes at points of contact. And he works *within* the subcultures as well.

Included among the subcultural communities served by the American police officer are those of the lower-class Negroes, lower-class whites, Chicanos (Mexican-Americans), Puerto Ricans, Chinese-Americans, Japanese-Americans, American Indians, and many smaller groups. It must also be mentioned that the superrich, the "old money," constitute a

People Who Don't Even Know You

nonconventional subculture, which at times presents law enforcement with problems few in number but of considerable perplexity.

Although it is often complained that police-community relations issues are reduced to race relations, it must be said that the everyday pressures of work make this tight focus inevitable. In the urban centers of the United States, with a few notable exceptions, the police-community relations issue *is* bound up with black-white interactions. However, the narrow focus need not be maintained. Police-community relations will be discussed in this chapter. The discussion will be carried on within a framework of subcultural relations which applies to all the minority populations living in the United States, even though much of the subcultural behavior dealt with is that of slum-dwelling Negroes.

The concepts of *subcultural behavior, culture shock, culture fatigue*, and *social change*, when considered from the perspectives of history and personal experience, can provide a fresh and more accurate insight into one's individual, personal position in the total scheme of things. It helps also in the making of judgments which lead to fewer, rather than more, tensions and difficulties on the job.

Policemen and Black People

Relations between the police and lower-class Negro residents of large urban areas of the northern and western United States have become increasingly and more visibly discordant in recent years. Ironically, this has occurred during a period of growing technical competence in law enforcement and greater police sensitivity to community reactions. But it has occurred also during a "revolution of rising expectations" among the urban poor, and curiously, the discord has been more pronounced and is most often found in the best cities of our country.

Police-community relations programs have achieved considerable popularity in recent years, but to many members of the community they seem to be "preaching to the converted," because of their limited reach. Even while Negro and police leaders meet to discuss large-scale problems, the individual police officer and the individual black man on the street find little improvement—more often a worsening—in their encounters.

These individual encounters obviously provide the medium in which the negative relationship is acted out, but consider for a moment that the factors that really underlie these harsh confrontations were probably operating long before the officer and black man came together. Unfortunately, most police-Negro encounters are predisposed to mutual hostility before they take place. This is *not* to suggest that the outcome of every contact must be inevitably negative; it is *not* to say that all of us—policemen and citizens—are trapped in a crystallized system of behavior within which we merely react in ways that are predetermined. However it is clear to any policeman or observer of police work that each police-citizen encounter begins with a lot of history behind it, that neither the officer nor the citizen enters the situation with a totally objective, assumption-free state of mind. Both are likely to carry into the meeting their personal quotas of "cultural baggage," those complex networks of knowledge, attitudes, and social awareness which are indispensable to everyday living. And to further complicate the conditions of the encounter, there are the personalities of the officer and the citizen, and the immediate conditions that brought them together.

It becomes increasingly apparent, however, that the factors of personality, individual intentions, and the conditions of meeting have less to do with the outcome of the encounter than the so-called cultural baggage of those involved. The forces of personality, intention, and immediate situation are overpowered by cultural forces which thrust upon the officer and the black man certain roles which become mutually antagonistic. Again, it must be said that unconscious behavior in response to social forces is not inevitable. However, unconscious reaction to those cultural urgings *is* exceedingly likely if the cultural urgings are not brought to the surface of the mind, clearly understood, and made part of the individual's total perspective of the conditions surrounding him. A number of factors have come together to complicate the everyday experiences of police officers and city residents. They include the internal migration patterns of the United States, which have formed the nation's cities; the historical relationships between Negroes and whites; the previously mentioned revolution of rising expectations among slum

People Who Don't Even Know You

dwellers; and the values and patterns of behavior dominant in two distinct segments of the larger American culture. These segments can properly be called the *lower-class Negro subculture* and the *police occupational subculture.*

Recent Urban Change

Intending to capture some of the flavor of city life in past generations and to compare that life-style with our personal knowledge of the present, we have already sampled a history of American urban development. It provides a factual backdrop for each of us, and has been presented to rid us of hazy, romantic notions about the past. The realities of the present can hardly compare favorably with an idealized past which never existed. But now, after having some sense of what urban living was like in the past, it might be well to bridge to the present and to attempt some understanding of the cities currently being served by our law enforcement organizations.

The Negro Exodus from the South

Between 1910 and 1963 it is estimated that more than 5,000,000 Negroes migrated from the Deep South, mostly to the large cities of the North and the West, in two distinctive patterns.[1] Between 1910 and 1940, about 1,750,000 migrants moved northward to the large cities directly in their paths ". . . from South Carolina to New York, from Georgia to Philadelphia, from Alabama to Detroit, and from Mississippi to Chicago."[2]

Between 1940 and 1963 migration largely followed the second pattern. During that period most of the 3,300,000 Negroes who left the South migrated to the western as well as to the northern cities. The Negro population outside the South has grown from 5 percent in 1860 to 10 percent in

[1] U.S. Department of Labor, *The Negroes in the United States* (Washington, D.C.: Government Printing Office, 1966), p. 1.

[2] Ralph Thomlinson, *Population Dynamics* (New York: Random House, Inc., 1965), pp. 219–20.

1910, 24 percent in 1950, and 40 percent in 1960.[3] Only 54 percent of the Negro population of this country now resides in the southern states.[4]

More often the reason for moving has been a desire to leave the South rather than a specific attraction of the destination. Ralph Tomlinson notes that the migrant's "knowledge of other parts of the country . . . is often imprecise and grossly inadequate. . . ." He finds the mood of migration captured in the line from Jelly Roll Morton's song, "Mississippi water tastes like turpentine, but Michigan water tastes like sherry wine."[5] In this same vein, and typical of migrant feelings is the letter of a migrant from Texas, who stated that he ". . . would like Chicago or Philadelphia but I don't Care where so long as I Go where a man is a man."[6]

But in his flight from the South, the Negro was unaware of the personal crisis that he had to face in the unsympathetic and impersonal environment of northern cities . . . and the absence of moral support of relatives and neighbors. . . . Primary forms of group control were dissolved and life became more secular. . . . Since tradition and sentiment no longer furnish a guide to living, the migrant is forced to make his own valuations of conduct and thereby develops 'rational' attitudes toward his environment. . . . For example, he learns that 'front' brings recognition, while a life lived according to the traditional values brings none of the rewards that the community values. Such an outlook on life easily leads to crime and other forms of antisocial behavior.[7]

Thus E. Franklin Frazier traced the severe cultural dislocation of lower-class Negroes to their pattern of migration from the South to the northern urban slum, with its absence of folk relationships and lack of traditional social controls.

The Quality of Life for In-migrants in Cities

In 1939 Edward I. Thorndike published the results of a

[3] *Ibid.*, pp. 444–45.

[4] U.S. Department of Labor, *Negroes in the United States*, p. 1.

[5] Thomlinson, *Population Dynamics*, p. 225.

[6] E. Franklin Frazier, *The Negro Family in the United States* (Chicago: University of Chicago Press, 1966), p. 227.

[7] *Ibid.*, pp. 227–29.

People Who Don't Even Know You

three years' study of 310 American cities. It was based upon the notion that "... the cities of the United States do differ enormously in many, and widely in almost all, of the features of qualities which are important for human living."[8] Thorndike analyzed differences in life-style among these several hundred cities in terms of factors relating to health, public educational opportunities, public recreation, economic well-being, creature comforts, literacy, and similar indicators of good conditions. The 310 cities of 30,000 or more population (in 1930) scored from 330 to 1110 points on a scale of 0 to 1541. Recently these "Goodness of Life" scores from the 1930s were compared with the rates of nonwhite in-migration for those same cities for the 1950–60 decade. The correlation coefficient was .81, indicating a very strong relationship between the quality of life in cities and their influx of southern rural black people.

So the Negro migrants went to the good cities; but there they discovered that northern and western cities did not dispense their "goodness of life" equally or randomly. "Social vacancies" existed—largely at the bottom of the socioeconomic scale—just as they had generations previously for the Irish, Germans, Italians, Poles, and other immigrant populations. There is clear evidence that Negroes fare better in earning power and education in the Thorndike high-score cities.[9] It is equally clear, however, that large numbers of unskilled, poorly educated in-migrants from the rural South, ignorant of city life, become the neighbors of settled second- and third-generation Negro residents who have done relatively well. One result of this is that the poorer, less capable in-migrants who came to the city expecting much—these expectations were reinforced by the relative success of established black residents—have been extremely frustrated by falling so short of their aspirations. Another result, given the nature of residential segregation in large cities, is that the long-time Negro residents have felt the full impact of the flood of socially unskilled migrants. Also, they are most often the victims of the crimes committed by the in-migrants and as the established black populations push outward, seeking ade-

[8]Edward L. Thorndike, *Your City* (New York: Harcourt Brace Jovanovich Inc., 1939), p. 5.

[9]Victor G. Strecher, "Police-Community Relations, Urban Riots, and the Quality of Life in Cities" (Doctor's thesis, Washington University [St. Louis, Mo.], 1968), pp. 106–7.

The Quality of Life for In-Migrants in Cities

quate living space, they are confronted on the one hand by white hostility to their expansion, and on the other by undesirable living conditions among the undereducated, socially different newcomers. This condition appears to be similar to the "lace curtain" and "shanty" Irish division of past generations. But the stigma of having black skin continues to block social assimilation, and it was social assmilation that eventually resolved the European immigrant crisis during the past 100 years.

The Lower-Class
Negro Subculture

Culture has been defined by Oscar Lewis, a well-known social scientist and author, as a "... design for living which is passed down from generation to generation.[10] This intergenerational design for living consists of behavior, goals, values, attitudes, personality patterns, and achievement levels, and it is a direct consequence of patterns of child-rearing and family life-style.[11]

The idea that a "culture of poverty" exists has been with us since 1961, when Oscar Lewis used the phrase.[12] Another expert, Catherine Chilman, feels that "... it would probably be more accurate to talk about the *sub*cultures of poverty ... because most of our poor would seem to subscribe to the 'middle-class American way' as ... a cultural ideal which most would accept, in theory and fantasy."[13] This last point —that the poor subscribe to middle-class norms, but behave in some other way—has been discussed by Lee Rainwater,[14] who suggests that a valid interpretation is found in Hyman Rodman's concept of a "lower-class value stretch," which permits the member of the lower-class to scale down a set of values to an operable level without abandoning the conven-

[10]Catherine S. Chilman, *Growing Up Poor* (Washington, D.C.: U.S. Department of Health, Education, and Welfare, 1966), p. 5.

[11]*Ibid.*, p. 5.

[12]*Ibid.*

[13]Chilman, *Growing Up Poor*, p. 6.

[14]Lee Rainwater, "The Problem of Lower Class Culture," Pruitt-Igoe Occasional Paper No. 8, Washington University, St. Louis, Mo., 1966, p. 5.

tional middle-class values of society.[15] Rainwater credits Rodman with avoiding

... the pitfall of making lower class persons out as "conceptual boobs" by not implying that (1) they are ignorant of or indifferent to conventional norms and values, or that (2) they persist in maintaining full-fledged allegiance to conventional norms despite their inability to achieve satisfactorily in terms of them.[16]

"It is now generally recognized that lower-class and middle-class families tend to raise their children and conduct their family relationships in quite different styles."[17] These different styles of child-rearing and family relationships do much to maintain behavior differing from conventional norms, behavior which is sufficiently distinctive to be called *subcultural*. Just what are the differences of behavior, goals, values, attitudes, personality patterns, and achievement levels of the lower-class Negro subculture?

Frazier calls attention to the pattern of family desertion by Negro men and estimates that women head the households in 10 to 30 percent of northern urban Negro families.[18] He calls this pattern an "inevitable consequence of the impact of urban life on the simple family organization and folk culture which the Negro has evolved in the rural South.[19]

Rainwater explores the view that in the lower-class subculture, scaled-down values and norms constitute "legitimate cultural alternatives" to conventional norms. His analysis centers on the heterosexual behavior—particularly premarital sexual intercourse, extramarital intercourse, and illegitimacy —of lower-class Negroes. He compares the *normative* expressions of housing project residents—"how things ought to be" —with their *existential* views—"how things are." Rainwater summarizes his findings in this way:

Lifelong marriage is the only really desirable way of living. ... Children should be born only in marriage relationships ... any

[15]Hyman Rodman, "The Lower Class Value Stretch," in *Planning for a Nation of Cities*, ed. S. B. Warner, Jr. (Cambridge, Mass.: The M.I.T. Press, 1966).

[16]Rainwater, "Problem of Lower Class Culture," p. 5.

[17]Chilman, *Growing Up Poor*, p. 5.

[18]Frazier, *Negro Family in the United States*, p. 246.

[19]*Ibid.*, p. 255.

kind of sexual relationship outside of marriage is a dangerous thing. . . . Sexual and procreative events outside of . . . marriage are not normative and they do involve costs . . . [however] reality makes it extremely difficult to live up to these norms. . . . The more impersonal socioeconomic forces and the intimate interpersonal forces of the community militate against living up to these norms and the majority of the population does not indeed live up to them.[20]

The result is that over a period of time, a set of more or less institutionalized alternatives has developed for adapting to the actual pressures under which men and women live. But these adaptations are not really satisfactory to those who make use of them, both because these people realize they have somehow fallen short of full moral status and feel themselves open to criticism, and because of the pains, frustrations, and tensions built into their way of living.

Boone Hammond has described "a 'contest system' which serves as a survival technique in the Negro lower-class subculture."[21] This system is one of nonphysical competition; in it the actors seek, through strategies of manipulation, to obtain the scarce goods of others. It is described as a "zero-sum" game because one person gains only that which another loses. In this system the two prime scarce objects are money and women, although women often represent another means of getting more money. "The ideal male type in this culture is the pimp or procurer who lives off the proceeds of seven or eight women, and never has to engage in the manual labor. . . ."[22] Hammond's major findings are that (1) the contest system causes an overriding atmosphere of skepticism and distrust, where an act of friendliness is construed as a prelude to one's being used or manipulated; (2) the methods of the contestants are at variance with conventional social norms; (3) the contest system pervades every phase of life and prevents the development of stable interpersonal relations and (4) inevitably intrudes between husbands and wives . . . "deferred gratifications are not seen to be of any utility. . . . In a culture where dreams never come true and middle class

[20]Rainwater, "Problem of Lower Class Culture," pp. 26–31.

[21]Boone E. Hammond, "The Contest System: A Survival Technique," Unpublished essay, Department of Sociology, Washington University, St. Louis, Mo., 1965, p. 1.

[22]Ibid., pp. 17–18.

People Who Don't Even Know You

oriented goals are seldom achieved, a man's thoughts do not go too far into the future."[23]

The City as Cauldron: Relative Deprivation

The urban disorders of recent years were followed by extensive studies of their causes. Among other things, these studies explored aspects of Negro life in cities which had been neglected until then. Separately and independently several research groups uncovered substantial support for the theory of *relative deprivation*.[24] Although the researchers rarely called this phenomenon by name, they described a condition lucidly explained in the following passage:

... people's attitudes, aspirations and grievances largely depend on the frame of reference within which they are conceived.... A person's satisfactions, even at the most trivial level, are conditioned by his expectations, and the proverbial way to make oneself conscious of one's advantages is to contrast one's situation with that of others worse off than oneself. The frame of reference can work in either of two ways.... Although at first sight a paradox, it has become a commonplace that steady poverty is the best guarantee of conservatism; if people have no reason to expect or hope for more than they can achieve, they will be less discontented with what they have, or even grateful simply to be able to hold on to it. But if, on the other hand, they have been led to see as a possible goal the relative prosperity of some more fortunate community with which they can directly compare themselves, then they will remain discontented with their lot until they have succeeded in catching up. It is this natural reaction which underlies the so-called "revolution of rising expectations."[25]

Ghetto Negroes are said to compare their lot with the affluent life-styles of whites, and of Negroes who have been able to leave the ghetto. In a sense they are forced into this

[23]*Ibid.*, pp. 11–13.

[24]This term was first used in *The American Soldier: Adjustment During Army Life* by Samuel A. Stouffer *et al.* (Princeton, N.J.: Princeton University Press, 1949).

[25]W. G. Runciman, *Relative Deprivation and Social Justice* (London: Routledge & Kegan Paul Ltd., 1966), p. 6.

comparison because "Through television . . . and the other media of mass communications, this affluence has been endlessly flaunted before the eyes of the Negro poor. . . ."[26]

Urbanologist Daniel P. Moynihan and the members of the McCone Commission view the riots, not as a simple consequence of poverty, but less directly, as a correlate of *perceived deprivation*. In introducing data from a 1964 statistical portrait of American cities prepared by the Urban League, the McCone Commission report posed the question, "Why Los Angeles?" The data established Los Angeles as first among 68 cities in quality of housing, employment, income, and seven other important factors affecting the quality of life for Negroes. The report states

The opportunity to succeed is probably unequaled in any other major American city. . . . Yet the riot did happen here, and there are special circumstances here which explain in part why it did. . . . In the last quarter century . . . the Negro population has increased almost tenfold from 75,000 in 1940 to 650,000 in 1965. Much of the increase came through migration from Southern states and many arrived with the anticipation that this dynamic city would spell the end of life's endless problems. To those who have come with high hopes and great expectations and see the success of others so close at hand, failure brings a special measure of frustration and disillusionment.[27]

In a series of widely published articles, Moynihan discussed the overwillingness of government bureaucrats and "liberals" to accept the "pathetically underfinanced programs which have normally emerged from Congress, and then to oversell them both to ourselves and those they are designed to aid. . . . We have tended to avoid evidence of poor results, and in particular have paid too little heed to the limited capacities of government bureaucracies to bring about social change."[28] Writing from a vantage point of personal involvement in the Kennedy Administration, Moynihan discussed government-planned social action as follows:

[26]National Advisory Commission on Civil Disorders, *Report* (New York: New York Times Company, 1968), p. 204.

[27]Governor's Commission on the Los Angeles Riots, *Violence in the City —An End or a Beginning?* (Los Angeles: State of California, Dec. 2, 1965), pp. 3–4.

[28]Daniel P. Moynihan, "Liberals Advised to Look Into Sources of Failures That Led to Race Rioting," *St. Louis Post-Dispatch*, August 7, 1967.

People Who Don't Even Know You

. . . our programs might have had far greater impact if only they had been of sufficient size, but they were not. . . . Anyone who was involved with the establishment of the War on Poverty knows that it was put together by fiscal mirrors; scarcely a driblet of new money was involved. . . . Huge-sounding bills were passed, but mini-appropriations followed . . . liberals both within and without the administration gave in to an orgy of tub thumping such as would have given pause to P. T. Barnum. . . . It does not follow that we raised hopes out of all proportion to our capacity to deliver on our promises, but if we did, and we must have, we have only ourselves to blame—ourselves and the federal bureaucracy.

Somehow liberals have been unable to acquire from life what conservatives seem to be endowed with at birth, namely a healthy skepticism of the powers of government agencies to do good. . . . As an instrument for providing services, especially to urban lower class Negroes, it [the federal government] is a highly unreliable device.[29]

Although the subject at hand is not urban disorders, there is clear relevance of these reports to our discussion of lower-class Negro behavior in large cities, and for their customary reaction to police uniforms.

The Police Subculture

A great majority of policemen are Caucasians, who have been reared in working-class or middle-class families. And unfortunately, the generalized pattern of residential segregation makes it likely that at the time of recruitment to police service, most of these young men know little more about the lower-class Negro subculture than they know about foreign cultures. Military service has afforded many young men a generous exposure to foreign cultures, but life in American cities normally provides few encounters with Negro communities. Relatively few white police recruits have been on social visits to Negro homes, and still fewer have had persisting friendships with black contemporaries. The point being stressed here is the *degree of separation* between the dominant conventional culture from which most policemen emerge and

[29]Daniel P. Moynihan, "Negro Poverty Deepening," *St. Louis Post-Dispatch*, August 9, 1967.

the black culture—particularly the lower-class or poverty-level Negro subculture. This almost complete separation of cultures, from birth through maturity, is powerfully significant for the officer's reactions when he first encounters Negro living patterns; this matter of personal reactions as it affects police work will be considered in detail later.

In addition to childhood and adolescent socialization into the conventional culture, the police recruit undergoes a process of occupational socialization, through which he becomes identified—by himself and his associates—as a policeman, and he begins to share all the perspectives relevant to the police role. Some years ago a book entitled *Boys in White* presented a model of an occupational subculture, medicine.[30] This model fits law enforcement equally as well. Much of the following section is adapted from that model.

The police subculture refers, first of all, to a set of group assumptions among policemen—assumptions about their work and their roles as officers. Secondly, there is "coherence and consistency" among the police perspectives, and those perspectives are related to the officer's role in the police organization. Responsibilities, duties, rights, and privileges are also part of the subcultural setting. "Because they all occupy the same institutional position, they tend to face the same kinds of problems, and these are the problems which arise out of the character of the position. . . . The opportunities and disabilities of the [*police*] *role* are decisive in shaping the perspectives [policemen] hold.' "[31] The concept of the police subculture emphasizes that policemen proceed beyond those perspectives learned during all the previous years before they entered law enforcement work. The press of new problems related to their work is far more decisive in shaping new outlooks than prior experiences, even though backgrounds may influence individual adjustments to the new police role. We use "police subculture" then, as a kind of shorthand term for the organized sum of *police perspectives*, relevant to the *police role*.[32]

Boys in White describes a number of perspectives of medical students toward medical practice and patients, drawn

[30]Howard S. Becker et al., *Boys in White* (Chicago: University of Chicago Press, 1961), p. 47.
[31]*Ibid.*, pp. 46–47.
[32]*Ibid.*, pp 4–7.

from medical culture. A few of these perspectives are given here, followed by transformation to make them appropriate to policemen. These perspectives provide considerable insight into the dimensions and texture of the occupational subculture.

the concept of medical responsibility pictures a world in which patients may be in danger of losing their lives and identifies the true work of the physician as saving those endangered lives. Further, where the physician's work does not afford (at least in some symbolic sense) the possibility of saving a life or restoring health through skillful practice . . . the physician himself lacks some of the essence of physicianhood.[33]

Transformed for applicability to the police occupation this passage reads

. . . the concept of police responsibility pictures a world in which the acts and intended acts of criminals threaten the lives or well-being of victims and the security of their property. The true work of the police officer is the protection of life and property by the intervention in, and solution of criminal acts. Further, where the policeman's work does not afford (at least in some symbolic sense) the possibility of protecting life or property by intervening in criminal acts, the police officer himself lacks some of the essence of police identity.

Those patients who can be cured are better than those who cannot. *Those cases which can be solved are better than those which cannot.* Students worry about the dangers to their own health involved in seeing a steady stream of unscreened patients, some of whom may have dangerous communicable diseases. *Policemen are concerned about personal hazards involved in approaching a steady stream of unknown persons, some of whom are wanted criminals, some of whom may have serious behavioral problems, and some possibly having intentions of causing them injury or even death because of circumstances unknown to the policemen. ,*

The most interesting and applicable medical perspective —one that resounds in the police world—is the following: "Perhaps the most difficult scenes come about when patients

[33] *Ibid.*, pp.. 316–20.

have no respect for the doctor's authority. Physicians resent this immensely."[34] The transformation is left to you.

The Professionalism Value
in the Police Subculture

Much of the present content of the police subculture has derived from the move to professionalize law enforcement. One of the consequences of the Spoils Era (1829–1883)[35] was a strong desire to eliminate the influence of politicians over the internal management of police departments. Political interference in police matters which had brought on this strong and enduring reaction included the manipulation of personnel, a practice which often resulted in promoting compliant, incompetent officers to executive rank. It also resulted in a dictation of enforcement policies; policemen were frequently required to overlook gambling and prostitution in establishments whose owners were heavy contributors to the political party controlling the executive or legislative unit of government.

Such experiences led to a powerful drive toward *autonomy* for the police, in the sense that the medical and legal professions are self-regulating, or autonomous. Unfortunately this laudable effort to elevate the ethical standards of the police service depended to a large extent on a model of autonomy which does not fit in with the American philosophy of government. The idea of each individual practitioner's being responsible for his own conduct and that there would be review by an organization of practitioners, is incompatible with the organizational structures and systems within which policemen work. There are civil administrative laws regulating conduct; executive branch public policies; police departmental policies, procedures, rules and regulations, supervision, command, and inspection; there is judicial review. Thus professional autonomy is not only not available to the patrolman, but neither is it available to the supervisor, commander, or executive.

[34]*Ibid.*, pp. 320–21.
[35]A. C. Germann, Frank D. Day, and Robert R. J. Gallati, *Introduction to Law Enforcement* (Springfield, Ill.: Charles C Thomas, Publisher, 1967), p. 68.

People Who Don't Even Know You

Beyond these immediate concerns for improved ethical standards, there was a tendency to isolate the factor of coldly efficient, technical competence as a major criterion of professionalism, and to judge police policy, action, and process on this basis. In this respect, several highly regarded law enforcement executives of the past generation were models of police professionalism and led in the movement for it. Theirs was a response to the problems of administering police services in a pluralistic society; such problems seemed to demand scrupulous attention to legal and administrative objectivity. It was also a response to the history of politics in law enforcement, and the professionalizers were justified in associating politics with corruption, incompetence, and maladministration. Thus, professionalism demanded responsiveness largely to the abstract criteria of ethics and technical competence. This in turn resulted in an occupational fixation upon *process*, or *technique*, to the exclusion of *function* or *goal orientation*. One of the most discernible trends in law enforcement has been the outright rejection of functions that are clearly aspects of community protection, and these functions have been rejected merely because the process or technique involved was not a traditional police method. Conversely, the police have taken on the most outlandish functions because they could be accomplished by means of traditional police procedures or because they required field forces such as the police could allocate to them.

Subcultural Perspectives of Policemen

Several of the police subcultural perspectives which are relevant to dealing with Negro slum dwellers are the following:

1. The officer is responsible for *maintaining order* in his patrol territory. There is supervisory, departmental, and general community pressure for orderliness and tranquility.
2. The policeman must be *respected*.
3. In every encounter the policeman must gain *control* of in the sense of initiating and orienting each part of the the situation and maintain that control; he must prevail,

The Police Subculture

encounter; psychological and strategic advantages must be maintained.

4. Incongruous activities or conditions must be investigated to determine whether the law is being violated. *Curiosity* and *suspiciousness* are valued traits in the police service; they are considered indispensable to craftsmanship; they shape the appropriate frame of mind for the officer as he goes about his work.

5. A general sense of social *appropriateness* is as much a part of the policeman's frame of reference as is the criminal law. From the earliest days of policing, the broad charge to the police to protect life and property and to preserve the peace has included maintenance of community order as conventionally defined. Public displays of certain human activities are to be curtailed: quarrels, drinking, sexual petting, loitering in large groups, loud conversation, boisterous joke telling, sitting on sidewalks, and dozens of other miscellaneous activities which offend the conventional sense of propriety.

6. Policemen share a general assumption that the amount of illegal activity, the harm to human beings, the loss of property, and the amount of disorderly activity far exceeds what comes to their attention. Part of their function is to seek out and deal with *elusive crime and criminals*.

There are, of course, numerous other elements in the total police perspective; however, these few will serve to highlight the particular occupation-oriented pressures on policemen in parts of the community which do not strongly hold middle-class or working-class values. These areas include the neighborhoods of lower-class Negroes and whites and also the habitat of the wealthy and superwealthy, especially the "old money."

Whenever a policeman works in a social setting greatly different from the one in which he was born and reared, he faces many of the same tensions and complexities as those encountered by foreign service personnel working for the first time in a strange country.

The Shock of Culture

In every society, people learn the behavior that is appropriate to them and that they may expect from others in an infinite number of situations in which they may find themselves. Differing

People Who Don't Even Know You

perceptions of role behavior frequently cause difficulties in inter-cultural settings because the members of each group are faced with unexpected behavior or with behavior that they feel is not appropriate to the setting. They are also handicapped by being unsure as to what is expected of them.[36]

For consideration of what happens to the policeman who is assigned to a neighborhood socially different from his own, the preceding paragraph can set the framework. It may be tentatively stated that police officers suffer *culture shock* during their early exposure to the lower-class Negro sub-culture. Culture shock has been defined as "an occupational disease of people who have been suddenly transplanted abroad."[37] The term has rarely been applied to police work, but there is a precise correspondence between the experiences of policemen and foreign service personnel under similar conditions.[38]

Culture shock is set in motion by the anxiety that results from losing all one's familiar cues. These cues include the thousand and one ways in which we orient ourselves to the situations of daily life: when to shake hands and what to say when we meet people, when and how much to tip, how to give orders to ser-vants, how to make purchases, when to accept and when to refuse invitations, when to take statements seriously, and when not to. Cues to behavior (which may be words, gestures, facial expressions, or customs) are acquired in the course of growing up and are as much a part of our culture as the language we speak. All of us depend for our peace of mind and our efficiency on hundreds of cues, most of which we do not carry on a level of conscious awareness.[39]

For the policeman, personal disorientation through the loss of familiar cues is due to unprecedented working prob-lems as well as to the cultural strangeness and resulting communications problems. But more about that later. At this point it is useful to recognize the stages and symptoms

[36]George M. Foster, *Traditional Cultures: and the Impact of Techno-logical Change* (New York: Harper & Row, Publishers, 1962), p. 130.

[37]Kalervo Oberg, quoted in Foster, *Traditional Cultures*, p. 187.

[38]This application of the culture shock concept was first established in Victor G. Strecher, "When Subcultures Meet: Police-Negro Relations," in *Law Enforcement Science and Technology*, ed. Sheldon Yefsky (Washington, D.C.: Thompson Book Co., 1967), pp. 701–7.

[39]Foster, *Traditional Cultures*, p. 188.

The Shock of Culture

of culture shock, for they are almost universally found among officers serving for the first time in urban slums. "Immunity to culture shock does not come from being broadminded and full of good will. These are highly important characteristics ... and they may aid in recovery, but they can no more prevent the illness than grim determination can prevent a cold. Individuals differ greatly in the degree to which culture shock affects them. A few people prove completely unable to make the necessary adjustments . . ."[40] [but most people recover fully].

There are four discernible stages in the culture shock syndrome.[41] The first is a kind of honeymoon period, lasting anywhere from a few days to several months, depending on circumstances. During this time the individual is fascinated by the novelty of the strange culture. He remains polite, friendly, and perhaps a bit self-effacing. The second stage begins when the individual settles down to a long-run confrontation with the real conditions of life in the strange culture, and he realizes fully that he needs to function effectively there. He becomes hostile and aggressive toward the culture and its people. He criticizes their way of life and attributes his difficulties to deliberate trouble making on their part; he seeks out others suffering from culture shock and, with them, endlessly belabors the customs and "shortcomings" of the local people. This is the critical period. Some never do adjust to the strange culture; they either leave the environment—voluntarily or involuntarily—or suffer debilitating emotional problems and, consequently become ineffective in their relations with the local population. In the third stage the individual is beginning to open a way into the new cultural environment. He may take a superior attitude to the local people, but he will joke about their behavior rather than bitterly criticize it. He is on his way to recovery. In the fourth stage the individual's adjustment is about as complete as it can get. He accepts the customs of the other culture as just another way of living.

Of course, this description of culture shock phases does not apply directly to law enforcement officers because with them the third and fourth stages do not always follow the first two. Foreign service agencies recognize, expect, and prepare for culture shock; they assume that it is a form of sociopsy-

[40] *Ibid.*, p. 189.
[41] Adapted from Foster, *Traditional Cultures*, pp. 189–92.

People Who Don't Even Know You

chological maladjustment which will respond to treatment (often informal). They expect that those affected will make the transition to satisfactory adjustment and effective cross-cultural relationships. This however, is not the experience in police departments, as will be discussed later in this chapter.

It should be stressed that the problems which lead the policeman into culture shock are real, not imagined. There is nothing quite so disruptive as a set of experiences which challenge one's working assumptions about the nature of the world and the people in it. Nor does the personal difficulty caused by the initial subcultural contact end the officer's problems of adjustment if he weathers the attack of culture shock. Recent experience indicates that later, more enduring intercultural tensions often follow the strains of early adjustment.[42]

A second major complex of reactions . . . can be summed up by the term "culture fatigue" (Guthrie 1963). This term refers to a phenomenon different from the "culture shock" experienced by many Americans immediately after they enter a new culture. . . . Culture fatigue is the physical and emotional exhaustion that almost invariably results from the infinite series of minute adjustments required for long-term survival in an alien culture. Living and working overseas generally requires that one must supply his automatic evaluations and judgments; that he must supply new interpretations to seemingly familiar behavior; and that he must demand of himself constant alterations in the style and content of his authority. Whether this process is conscious or unconscious, successful or unsuccessful, it consumes an enormous amount of energy, leaving the individual decidedly fatigued.

One effect of culture fatigue, a tendency toward negative interpretations of all foreign culture, has lead American business and government personnel in one nation to regard close family ties as "clannishness," personal sensitivity as "sulkiness," avoiding unpleasant subjects as "dishonesty," and lavish hospitality as "wastefulness."[43]

Summary

To summarize: the exodus of approximately 5,000,000 Negroes from the rural South and their migration largely

---

[42]Robert B. Texter, *Cultural Frontiers of the Peace Corps* (Cambridge, Mass.: The M.I.T. Press, 1966), pp. 48–49.
[43]*Ibid.*, p. 49.

into the metropolitan areas of the North and West had enormous consequences for those cities. It is valid to refer to them as *target cities* or *receiving cities* and to describe their characteristics because the southern black migrant patterns were quite specific. A *target city*, then, could be portrayed as follows: it is a large city; although its nonwhite population may have been either large or small in 1950, during the next ten years an influx of in-migrants from southern farmlands significantly raised the nonwhite composition of the central city. An already high level of residential segregation increased further, and population density increased along with it. But the target city had long been one of the good cities to live in. During the 1930s it had more available jobs at better pay, fewer infant deaths, more libraries and museums, better schools and teachers, less extreme poverty, more property owners, and fewer homicides than cities of comparable size. And the Negroes came in greater numbers to this kind of city to share in those good things. Some long-time Negro residents of such cities had become economically successful, and some of the newcomers joined them. Few Negroes, however, achieved levels of success comparable to the whites. And many Negroes, both long-time residents and migrants, remained poor. There was a dramatic chasm between the job holders who were earning good pay and those without skills, the unemployed. Contrasts in the target city are great, and they are visible to both the affluent and the poor. During the past several years the impact of perceived differences has undoubtedly been sharpened by explicit discussion.

The Negro exodus resulted in patterns of social adaptations unlike either those of the folk culture of rural southern life or of preexisting urban northern Negro life in the receiving areas. These social adaptations—sometimes called survival techniques—which rendered Negro life at least functionally possible in urban slums produced behavior patterns within the Negro community which are clearly different from the conventional norms of the larger society. Incidentally, these conventional norms were expressed by lower-class Negro residents as "how things ought to be." Given the limited social resources and realities of lower-class Negro life, there evolved a set of scaled-down subcultural norms. These were substituted for the conventional norms of society because they were workable.

Dissonance, or disharmony, exists in the lower-class

People Who Don't Even Know You

88

Negro's simultaneous awareness of the conventional social norms of behavior and the substituted norms by which he lives. There is also dissonance in his knowledge that this subcultural behavior does not work out nearly as well as most residents say it does. The means of reducing this dissonance are to reject the conventional cultural goals and the legitimate means of accomplishing them. (Often this is done in an outburst which indicates the intensity of the internal conflict.) Then one attaches allegiance to other goals and means which bring behavior and norms into alignment. This, however, is a tensely balanced solution for the lower-class Negro.

Enter the policeman, who has problems of his own. He is recruited from the middle and working classes, and as a result of historical racial segregation patterns, knows almost nothing of the Negro poverty subculture. His occupational socialization produces a self-concept centered upon crime fighting and life protection, and also a set of subcultural perspectives which tend to reject roles dissonant with this self-concept. Yet every police officer discovers that his radio assignments break down to approximately 80 percent minor regulatory functions or service calls and 20 percent serious crimes. When the latter is the case, he is quickly replaced by investigative personnel so that he can return to his radio for additional service calls. In addition to the initial surprises about the nature of his work, the policeman who is assigned to a predominantly lower-class Negro neighborhood experiences a culture shock reaction to the social strangeness, the loss of familiar cues and symbols, and his inability to interact spontaneously with the Negro residents. Neither his conventional values nor the perspectives he has been given in early training—responsibility for order, demand for respect, situational control, suspiciousness, and application of conventional appropriateness—seem to guide him into the most sensible and productive courses of action. Upon discovering that his twenty-one or more years of social experience and the added perspective of his new role utterly fail him in his first few encounters with lower-class Negro behavior and problems, he becomes anxious and frustrated. After the first few unsatisfactory encounters, the officer begins to anticipate unpleasant interactions with lower-class black people—and then, with all black people, because he is unable to make social distinctions within the Negro population. It is natural for the officer to react aggressively to this frustrating experience. This be-

Summary

89

comes his stage two of culture shock; he welcomes any opportunity to gripe about the slum dwellers—their appearance, lack of cleanliness, affinity for big cars, inedible foods; almost any aspect of Negro life will do—and as he goes about his duties, his feelings are virtually impossible to conceal. In fact, the very nature of culture shock makes him want to display something of what he is feeling; after all, he holds these people responsible for his new problems.

What comes across clearly to the black resident in this policeman's territory is a harsh, moralistic indictment of the Negro way of life, seen in the words, expressions, and gestures of the officer. Remember this Negro man has not been insulated from American aspirations for success; he has come to this big city which seemed to promise so much, and has found no way to even begin to climb upward from his low point in the social system. He knows how he lives, and he needs nobody to tell him that his standards fall below conventional levels; he settles for less in every way, including what he demands of himself; but he feels deep dissatisfaction, frustration, and a certain self-condemnation when he thinks about it for too long. For this man, the policeman's visible feelings while in culture shock result in reactivating and intensifying all his personal regrets and frustrations about the same aspects of his life-style. For the moment the policeman's reaction becomes an embodiment of the hostile, superior stare of middle-class society—of those who have made it, and have it made.

One of the difficulties on the police side of the relationship is the absence of measures to conquer culture shock. During its severe phase its symptoms are not relieved; there is no minimizing of its adverse effects upon police-civilian relations during this time. And nothing is done to bring about a complete recovery. It is not surprising that culture shock and culture fatigue are not recognized in American police departments. After all, it is not customary to think of large numbers of our city residents as members of another culture. And yet it has been found that Peruvians sent to work in isolated communities in their own country suffered greatly from culture shock.[44] Actually this is a form of *subculture* shock similar to what is found among policemen. Make no

---

[44] Paul L. Doughty, "Pitfalls and Progress in the Sierra Peruvian," in Robert B. Textor, ed., *Cultural Frontiers of the Peace Corps* (Cambridge, Mass.: The M.I.T. Press, 1966), pp. 221–39.

People Who Don't Even Know You

mistake about it: the average young white police recruit will experience culture shock soon after reporting for duty in a black slum, and unfortunately, he will find few resources to help him out of it. In the average police department, the symptoms of culture shock in young policemen appear to be considered a coming of age, a first hard contact with the realities of big-city policing—a contact in which the recruit is learning the proper way to regard the behavior of lower-class blacks. Emotional support from experienced associates often comes from men who have also experienced culture shock and have progressed into culture fatigue. This support is less likely to sensitize the recruit and guide him toward a resolution of his conflict than to toughen him to the long-run prospect of dealing with lower-class behavior, and to crystallize this toughness. This creates a dilemma for the young officer, because as has been stated of those in culture shock, "In the final analysis our feeling of professional adequacy depends on how our colleagues evaluate us."[45]

In the absence of departmental efforts to alleviate culture shock and lessen culture fatigue, there is much that can be done by the recruit himself to find his way out of this disoriented, uncomfortable state. The final chapter will discuss these means.

[45]Foster, Traditional Cultures, p. 192.

The
Daily
Performance

A police administrator of extraordinary talent once offered this succinct advice for young policemen: "Always know who you are, where you are, and what you are doing there."[1] Everything presented so far has in a sense been directed toward those ends; it has been designed to give you some purchase on the here and now. If you understand the derivation of the police function and role, have some awareness of social change and its complex causes, see behind the myths of the "good" and "safe" cities of the past, gaining a more realistic sense of what has preceded us; and glimpse the powerful cultural forces which underlie even simple encounters between policemen and individual citizens—you will be pointed in the direction of conscious *deliberate action* as contrasted with unthinking *reflex action*. (The latter has the merit of speed but the liability of a very low batting average.) A man who commands deep historical and social perspectives and who understands something of political philosophy and ideology is not easily frightened by political catch phrases. He is not impressed by garden variety "viewing-with-alarm." Nor is he stampeded into frenzied action by accusations of police failure because of crime rate increases.

These crime rate increases, it should be noted, hardly match bygone days of crime, corruption, and human misery. Perhaps our cyclic panic reactions occur largely because we have convinced ourselves that man *is* a perfectible being and that we are truly making progress (change is often mistaken for progress); then, a generation later, we find ourselves at the same point, believing we have fallen back after having

[1] Chief of Police Curtis Brostron (St. Louis, Mo., Police Department) to the author, 1965.

climbed a great distance. It is more probable that most of our "progress" is simply nonadvantageous *change* and our periodic "regressions" mean that we are holding our own. In an age which places high value on miracle workers and instant success, perhaps it is not fashionable to suggest much scaled-down aspirations; however, that is precisely what the present chapter does.

Role Perspectives: Imperatives and Self-Determination

An important fact that you, as a policeman on the street, must never lose sight of is: *The police-community relationship must be viewed as an essential condition—but an insufficient one—for the practice of your occupation.* That is, your craftsmanship cannot be fully effective in the absence of a sound police-community relationship, but on the other hand, excellent community relations will not make up for a deficiency in your personal on-the-job skills. Your prime imperative, your major necessity, is that of fulfilling your role. Other considerations, however important they may be, must fit in with that prime concern; they must contribute to achieving it. The maintenance of favorable relations with your clientele—the entire public—will be treated as one part of your overall job performance. But, as the historical, social, and interpersonal sketches have indicated, good intentions and a smile won't help you make it; just as a doctor's smile is no substitute for antitoxin and an engineer's agreeable personality does not compensate for a structure weakened because he agreed to a client's unwise economies.

To fulfill your role you will need a workable set of concepts—what I prefer to call a *working frame of reference.* But synthesizing or building such a frame of reference for practical, everyday application is a tough assignment. Yet if you do not do so, you are forced to accept the *gut reaction* and *situational cleverness* as general approaches to problem solving, with all their side effects, accumulated error, and potential for compounded, magnified difficulties. Too simple solutions to human problems have left a historical trail of blundering catastrophe in the form of "logical" extremism, devaluation of individual worth, human casualties, and at the end, discredited leadership.

Your working frame of reference will require some sacrifice of neatness and simplicity, because the social world is neither neat nor simple, and your working assumptions must, above all, deal with the real world. The early chapters of this book can be regarded as a small input to your personal data bank, a set of categories to help guide you through the social minefields in your personal application of police skills.

Your relationships with members of the community must flow from a sense of craftsmanship, which is made up of personal skills and of deeply informed perspectives on the human condition and the effects of deliberate action. For you, this compound of perspective and craftsmanship, which may be termed professionalism, *is the essence of police-community relations.*

Learning and Making the Role

A previous chapter went into the idea of the police sub-culture and the process whereby a recruit gains his place in it. It was pointed out that young policemen learn the solutions (perspectives) which have been collectively worked out by innumerable officers who have gone before them, through a process of trial and error rather than of conscious design. It was also stated that this period of apprenticeship, of role learning, confronts the recruit with many simultaneous pressures which urge him to accept *some* perspective or other. The unsettling quality of those early days of initiation into the police occupation is perhaps difficult to remember, but go back for a moment to your earliest thoughts about entering law enforcement. Where were you? What were you doing? *How did you regard police work? What was your concept of a policeman?* What *part* of police work were you thinking of? In those days before you knew a lot about law enforcement, *what police role was central in your thoughts?*

Now allow yourself to re-create your first few days, weeks, and months as a police recruit. Try to remember the impact of your first exposures to the work itself—how you spent your time out on the street, either on foot or in a patrol car. Try to recall how much of this you anticipated before joining the department and how much was entirely unexpected. Where did your police *role*, your *identity* come from: your training? your first partner? trial and error? deliberate decisions on your part resulting from experience?

Once initiation into a subcultural occupation has begun, the undertow of process makes difficult this kind of recall and analysis. But the effort is well justified by the results. They offer you some personal choices among all the firm, unyielding demands of the new role—some possibilities of self-determination for you in the police role, which might go unnoticed if you do not consciously seek them out with at least half an idea of what might be found.

Personal Style and Effectiveness

A matter of central interest at this point is discovering every inch of latitude and flexibility within the system, all lapses of tradition which permit you some individual, personal development of technique—which allow, in a word, your growth of *style*. This *style* will be generated out of your perspectives, or working assumptions, your technical police skills, and your personality. As such, it will be unique, because no other human being can have precisely the same combination of knowledge, abilities, and attributes. In that sense, your individuality will be assured if you give yourself the opportunity to learn what is to be known, and to develop fully. But you must be cautious. All too frequently, young officers in a hurry to climb through the ranks fasten their attention on one or another of the gaudy, attention-getting styles seen in any large police department—for example, the "tough cop" role, which fulfills a limited function in connection with professional hoodlums. This is, however, a high-risk role, available to a limited few, and it is common to find large numbers of aspiring young officers who fail in the attempt.

In mapping out a strategy for your career development, by all means attend to the matter of personal style, but don't rush it. Let it evolve out of a thoroughgoing approach to your vocation. And as you proceed through the first few years, give some attention to the remaining sections of this book.

All of them are relevant to your maintaining the most flexible of relationships with all *others* so that your technical skills may be used to their greatest effectiveness.

Crime-fighting Plus
80 Percent: Adjustment
to Your Job

From the historical accounts of policing in North America, it may be concluded that there has never really been a progression away from crime fighting and toward general service functions, as police folklore would have it. From the earliest days, it is clear, those appointed to law enforcement positions were charged with solving all of the safety and security problems of the community as well as with enforcing laws. And security problems have changed. Indian attacks, wild bears on Main Street, witchcraft, and wife kissing in public are no longer prime concerns of law enforcement; however, crimes of all kinds, the safe movement of traffic, public drunkenness, lost children, prostitution, peace disturbances, domestic quarrels, and major civil disorders have continued from earliest colonial days to the present. There are also new public safety problems; these include experimentation with drugs, accidents involving radioactive materials, massive urban changes, and tensions related to three powerful forces: the population explosion, the information explosion, and the mobility explosion.

A fundamental matter for every police officer is coming to grips with his role in the community, arriving at a self-concept. If a man persists in identifying himself as primarily a crime fighter when in fact his function has never been more than 20 percent crime fighting and when his daily experience does not support this self-concept, it is inevitable that he will experience what is technically called *cognitive dissonance*, that is holding two conflicting bits of information in mind at the same time. Cognitive dissonance causes tension and discomfort because there is a nagging, subconscious struggle to resolve the conflict of information. In most cases the dissonance is gradually resolved by the officer's denying the validity of and disbelieving one of the bits of information. He either comes to redefine his role and function as a police officer, *or* he arrives at the belief that he is not really per-

The Daily Performance

forming police work as it once was and should still be. In the latter case, the officer is likely to be very unhappy in patrol work; he will probably desire very much to become a detective, whose work is more truly crime fighting. Of course this form of cognitive dissonance would not arise in the first place if men entering police work were not recruited and motivated by romantic but inaccurate definitions of their future roles. If they were reliably informed instead and then trained in accord with the police function as it exists, rather than as it is desired, there would be no problem.

The Only World We Have: Remembering the Lessons of History

Our religious, ethical, and political beliefs tend toward the proposition that man is a perfectible being, spiritually if not physically. However, the person who deals daily with human failings—whether a policeman, psychiatrist, or marriage counselor—jeopardizes his own emotional and mental health if he clings too tightly to this vision of trouble-free man and, by extension, trouble-free society. Neither exists, and for the realistic enforcer of the law, neither should be expected or even hoped for.

What you, as a policeman, *can* expect and hope for during your career must be a product of your informed, skeptical, honest perspective of your working place—urbanized society. And your perspective of the present-day community depends upon your having an equally thorough understanding of the past and the present. Only by extending your knowledge beyond personal experience and what can be learned from the oldsters, can you hope to escape a narrow interpretation of current conditions. Those in every generation who deplore the decay of morality, the demise of respect for policemen, the loss of respect for authority in general, the lack of consensus in human affairs, and the sudden loss of security in our cities have simply not paid attention to the lessons of the past.

Certainly change occurs; both cyclic change, in which history appears to repeat itself with minor variations and permanent, cumulative change, which presents the world with new and unique conditions. But change nearly always brings effects both beneficial and detrimental to the quality of human life. They are rarely as bad as the viewers-with-alarm would have it nor as rosy as the technology glamorizers claim.

The public service or law enforcement perspective which emerges from these understandings of present and past will vary from man to man, but it should squarely confront the following observations.

1. Human groups, whether large or small, are subject to internal and external insecurities, which are largely the products of human behavior. Throughout history, group insecurities and the behavior which produced them have brought about responses of group leadership or institutions intended to manage the tensions and behavior.

2. In comparatively recent times, managing behavior and group insecurities has become increasingly the business of institutions, particularly governmental and educational institutions. It has been less influenced by moral consensus; that is, human regulation has largely moved from the sacred toward the secular domain.

3. Change in human living patterns occurs as a result of the interactions of values, cultural institutions, social structures, technology, and the environment. Most change probably results from the combined effects of these factors upon the behavior of millions of persons, both as individuals and in their many groupings. Some of the resulting change is desirable to most persons; some is deplorable and frightening to virtually everyone. But, given the dimensions and momentum of its underlying forces, change has not yet become subject to human management and control, despite wishful beliefs to the contrary.

4. Styles of human life appear to change considerably from one generation to the next. Much of this change is regarded by short-run observers as either progress or social decay. Evidence is increasing, however, that much of the change in life-styles actually consists of change in the visibility of human behavior and change in attitudes toward that behavior, rather than in change in the kind or amount of behavior. This is particularly apparent when, as in the case of human sexual activity, powerful values interact with a form of behavior.

5. Paramount and substantial change, rather than cyclic and seeming change, may be found in certain recent social responses to technological innovations, especially in transport and communication. As a result of some innovations, change has apparently speeded up. This

The Daily Performance

has made critically important the long-standing time lag in the response of institutions to new demands made upon them. These institutions—the government, schools, churches, and labor unions—have not yet adapted to the change of pace. Law enforcement, always involved with the working out of conduct standards and social response to deviations from them, is very much affected by the newly critical importance of lag in its response to new conditions.

6. The design of democracy in the United States imposes special demands upon police officers in this country. In the pull between security and individual freedom, we tend slightly toward the side of *inefficient* social control —purposely. Those in law enforcement who find this difficult to accept should review their commitment to constitutional government. Those who cannot accept this factor of inefficiency to the extent that personal freedom may require it should not endure the frustrations of a law enforcement career.

When policemen gain the historic and contemporary perspectives, they lose both the security and insecurity which result from ignorance. The security is a form of false confidence, which literally sprays the man's environment with negative side effects as he blunders about in his sensitive and important work. The insecurity represents a tendency to gut react and stampede with others who are insecure when politically and socially sensitive catch words are attached to ordinary forms of social change or to harmless unconventional behavior. Recognizing true social hazards and subversion— which indeed exist—is not work for men who suffer from tunnel vision. Neither is it work for those who reason from insufficient or unverified information or who know what is best for everybody else. In America such men were not meant to be part of the law enforcement system.

Surviving at Low Cost: Getting Through Culture Shock and Culture Fatigue

The first and most essential step in working through *culture shock* is to anticipate it; the second is to recognize it when the symptoms appear. As discussed in the previous chapter, police departments do not recognize or treat culture

Personal Style and Effectiveness

shock in young policemen; each officer is therefore left to manage as well as he can. This makes recognizing the symptoms of culture shock more difficult, simply because its effects focus the attention of those afflicted with it on almost any explanation of their problems other than the obvious one— their personal maladjustment. Culture shock provides its own camouflage; thus, the condition often has to be called to the sufferer's attention by a colleague. This informal helping technique is not found in American police agencies, but the pattern would be rapidly established if young officers began to watch for symptoms of culture shock in each other and if they began to help one another recognize and work through this difficult period of adjustment. Also important would be the recognition of *culture fatigue* in the more experienced officers, a condition which makes it most difficult for them to assist their younger colleagues through the culture shock syndrome. Culture fatigue in mature officers should not be accepted by the newer men as an appropriate and permanent adjustment to the more unconventional social groups of the community.

Once culture shock has been recognized through its symptoms, what may be done about it?

1. First of all, seek support from your contemporaries. In any case, your anxiety will have been noticed.
2. Be candid about your feelings with your close associates but only away from public hearing.
3. During the period of adjustment while you are seeking the support of other officers, avoid all forms of spontaneous reaction to the subcultural groups of your community. This is difficult because your reactions of frustration, contempt, impatience, and sometimes fear are likely to show in your speech, gestures, eyes, and general mannerisms. To get through this phase of culture shock, cultivate a controlled outward manner, and discipline yourself to maintain that manner in public. But when you are alone, relax. Feel assured that the need for the pose will eventually pass and that you will develop the ability to deal spontaneously and naturally with most community groups.
4. Systematically inform yourself about subcultural styles of life, even though initially they appear to be unattractive, careless, dirty, immoral, unconventional, or otherwise alien to your own way of life. Don't be satisfied with one or two glimpses of other life-styles. Defer your judgments until you have explored them in considerable

The Daily Performance

detail. Always look for logical explanations of behavior, and don't accept what you hear from members of the subcultural groups or from other policemen without considering it carefully and critically. Get a number of versions, compare them, observe matters at first hand, and decide for yourself which explanations best fit your observations.

5. Upon joining the police department, don't assume that a personal attitude of goodwill, social awareness, or confidence will get you safely past culture shock. These traits may prepare you to more easily accept help from other officers when your anxiety becomes apparent, but they will not immunize you to culture shock. Often when they are confronted with the need to fulfill the police function on a day-to-day basis, those most inclined to take a liberal view toward the behavior of others experience the greatest maladjustment.

6. When your culture shock becomes focused on one community group, investigate, in great detail, at least one aspect of that group's way of life—its religious beliefs and pattern of worship, its art, music, code of conduct, or peculiarities of family life. Unless your prior knowledge was unusually complete, you will be astonished by the detail and intricacy of what formerly appeared to be merely "different," or subconventional behavior or life-style.

With help, most young policemen should be able to weather culture shock. They will then be in a position to settle down to providing good police service in any part of the community. However, the later, longer-lasting problem of culture fatigue still must be faced. Personal adjustments to the long-run pressures of culture fatigue may be regarded as "making peace" with the subcultural groups in your community. This involves "accepting the . . . culture in the sense of becoming emotionally capable of living with it relatively comfortably. . . ."[2]

Because for policemen culture shock and culture fatigue are not merely related to casual contact with subcultural groups but more specifically to the need to supply police service to these groups, the working out of personal maladjustment problems has to be accomplished in terms of getting the job done. Said in another way: a personal solution

[2] Robert B. Textor, ed., *Cultural Frontiers of the Peace Corps* (Cambridge, Mass.: The M.I.T. Press, 1966), p. 220.

Personal Style and Effectiveness

which does not fit the law enforcement function is not useful, because the policeman is not free to modify his role. Or is he?

Previously it was mentioned that police work, despite its requirements, rules, regulations, policies, and procedures. continues to leave to the individual officer considerable discretion in how to deal with specific cases. Following are a few suggestions which might be helpful in the process of long-term subcultural adjustments.

1. Learn to think in terms of problems rather than techniques or rigid procedures. Consider each assignment in terms of the basic police function—the protection of life and property and the preservation of tranquility. Next, consider the subcultural setting of your work: Who is to be served? What result will provide the best solution with a minimum of side effects? What are the long-run implications of doing it that way?
2. Consider *how* as well as *what* you do in response to a call for service in subcultural neighborhoods. In determining the reactions of others, style is often the decisive feature in your action.
3. If you are at a complete loss and feel unable to cope with your culture shock and fatigue, look about you for an officer who deals successfully with community subcultures (who gets the job done competently, minimizes negative reactions, appears unflappable, and maintains an even disposition). Copy his official behavior. At work "put on" his personality and hold to the role. In time this role will become an effective part of you. But be certain that you are emulating the right man. Examine his actions from all sides.

Wearing the Role:
Appearances and Manners

As a police officer you operate on three different levels (1. being seen, 2. momentary face-to-face encounters, and 3. long exposure to a citizen through extended service) and present yourself to the public in three separate ways. The first mode of presentation is the most superficial but the most widespread of the three—that of merely *being seen* by great numbers of persons. It is worth noting that this most frequent exposure offers members of the community the least opportunity for a fair appraisal of you as a policeman. And yet they do appraise. They judge you in your role, and they add this casual observation to their previous attitudes and opinions about the police. In a brief moment, the citizen observes the state of your uniform; your posture, outward manner and rate of movement; your facial expression; and your general conduct in the police role. There is no way on earth to correct or change the impression you create in this way in the minds of thousands of people. You have no access to them. During your career in a large city, you will never talk with more than a handful of them. Whenever you are seen by others, therefore, present yourself as you want to be known.

The second mode of presentation is the brief, face-to-face encounter with hundreds of people who require police service. Rarely do these meetings last long, rarely do they afford the civilian or policeman more than a glimpse of the other's role. One is a client with a problem, the other is there to help with it. Seldom does a personal consideration enter into this relationship. The citizens who see you in this second setting receive a somewhat greater opportunity to evaluate you. Not only do they see you at close range for visual appraisal; they see your reaction to their problems, they hear you speak, and they receive a sharply etched impression of you in the police role. They are fewer in number than the mere observers, but they form a more substantial opinion from their greater exposure to your appearance, conduct, and speech. Again, this opinion cannot be easily undone.

The third mode of presentation is relatively rare for most policemen; it consists of serving the needs of a citizen over quite a long period of time. It enables him to see something of the officer's personality, as it were, by peering around the edges of the police role. In a long career you will experience this kind of contact a number of times but seldom in the course of patrolling in a vehicle. When this kind of relationship does arise, the citizen has an opportunity to form a more valid appraisal of you than in either of the two previous situations. If this deeper relationship were common for policemen, their appearance and approach to clientele would lose much of their importance. The man behind the uniform and man behind the role would easily outweigh the superficial judgments based upon his appearance or approach only. Unfortunately, this is not the case. All but a tiny part of the public will develop their impressions of the police and their attitudes toward them as a result of seeing many many officers, talking with a handful during their lives, and perhaps knowing one or more policemen personally.

A special category within the second mode of presentation is that of police conduct on the telephone. In this case, even appearance is not working for you (or against you); voice, diction, reaction to the citizen's call, approach to the problem, and basic etiquette are the criteria of judgment. Here again, negative evaluations cannot be reversed. The police telephone response can easily predispose a complainant to a favorable or unfavorable reception of the radio car officers who later respond to this request. Those who neglect telephone courtesy will not overcome the deficiency in police image through the correctness of their uniform and their approach to service calls. As a result the work, even when it is well performed, becomes harder to accomplish.

All of the People, All of the Time: Everybody Belongs to a Minority Group

A previous chapter dwelled at length upon the interaction between policemen and lower-class blacks. It highlighted the factor of role playing by each. The discussion could have dealt with a variety of other minority or subcultural groups, but because of the immediacy or relevance of the issues, information is more readily available for this group. On the other hand, by choosing one subcultural group for the purposes of this book the matter of police-community relations might be erroneously portrayed in the narrow setting of race relations or, more specifically, Negro-white relations. This would be a major error because by adopting so limited a perspective, the police can greatly endanger their community function and responsibility. There are many other categories of subcultural and special-interest groups which call for particularized police-community relationships and thus which constitute special parts of the policeman's environment. Racial ethnic, and religious groups usually represent the special needs of their membership through some recognized leadership. Law enforcement policies and practices, especially at the operational level, are often relevant concerns of these groups because their ways of behaving—in which they may take deep pride—frequently differ from conventional behavior in harmless ways or sometimes in ways that irritate the more sensitive of our conventional citizens. Protecting subcultural groups and resolving minor problems at their points of contact with the dominant community body often become police assignments. A thorough understanding of the rich complexity of our cities, of our governmental heritage and its deep challenges for law enforcement, and of the difficult intergroup and interpersonal relationships that come with the police role —all of these are part of knowing the environment of law enforcement.

All of the People, All of the Time

Bibliography

BECKER, HOWARD S., et al., *Boys in White*. Chicago: University of Chicago Press, 1961.

CHILMAN, CATHERINE S., *Growing Up Poor*. Washington, D.C.: U.S. Department of Health, Education, and Welfare, 1966.

COSTELLO, AUGUSTINE E., *Our Police Protectors: History of the New York Police*. New York: Police Pension Fund, 1885.

FLINN, JOHN J., *History of the Chicago Police*. Chicago: Police Book Fund, 1887.

FOSTER, GEORGE M., *Traditional Cultures: and the Impact of Technological Change*. New York: Harper & Row, Publishers, 1962.

FRAZIER, E. FRANKLIN, *The Negro Family in the United States*. Chicago: University of Chicago Press, 1966.

GERMANN, A. C., FRANK D. DAY, and ROBERT R. J. GALLATI, *Introduction to Law Enforcement*. Springfield, Ill.: Charles C Thomas, Publisher, 1957.

GLAAB, CHARLES N., ed., *The American City: A Documentary History*. Homewood, Ill.: Dorsey Press, 1963.

GOVERNOR'S COMMISSION ON THE LOS ANGELES RIOTS, *Violence in the City—An End or A Beginning?* Los Angeles: State of California, Dec. 2, 1965.

HALE, GEORGE W., *Police and Prison Cyclopaedia*. Boston: W. L. Richardson Co., 1893.

HAMMOND, BOONE E., "The Contest System: A Survival Technique," Unpublished essay, Department of Sociology, Washington University, St. Louis, Mo., 1965.

HEAPS, WILLARD A., *Riots, U.S.A., 1765–1965*. New York: The Seabury Press, Inc., 1966.

LANE, ROGER, *Policing the City: Boston 1822–1885*. Cambridge, Mass.: Harvard University Press, 1967.

MEASE, JAMES, "Municipal Services," in *The American City:*

A Documentary History, ed. Charles N. Glaab. Homewood, Ill.: Dorsey Press, 1963.

MOYNIHAN, DANIEL P., "Liberals Advised to Look Into Sources of Failures That Led to Race Rioting," *St. Louis Post-Dispatch*, August 7, 1967.

————, "Negro Poverty Deepening," *St. Louis Post-Dispatch*, August 9, 1967.

MYRDAL, GUNNAR, *An American Dilemma*. New York: Harper & Row, Publishers, 1944.

NATIONAL ADVISORY COMMISSION ON CIVIL DISORDERS, *Report*. New York: New York Times Company, 1968.

RAINWATER, LEE, "The Problem of Lower Class Culture," Pruitt-Igoe Occasional Paper No. 8, Washington University, St. Louis, Mo., 1966.

RODMAN, HYMAN, "The Lower Class Value Stretch," in *Planning for a Nation of Cities*, ed. S. B. Warner, Jr. Cambridge, Mass.: The M.I.T. Press, 1966.

RUNCIMAN, W. C., *Relative Deprivation and Social Justice*. London: Routledge & Kegan Paul Ltd., 1966.

SAVAGE, EDWARD H., *Police Records and Recollections, or Boston by Daylight and Gaslight for Two Hundred and Forty Years*. Boston: John P. Dale & Co., 1873.

STOUFFER, SAMUEL A., et al., *The American Soldier: Adjustment During Army Life*. Princeton, N.J.: Princeton University Press, 1949.

STRECHER, VICTOR G., "Police-Community Relations, Urban Riots, and the Quality of Life in Cities" (Doctor's thesis, Washington University, St. Louis, Mo., 1968).

SZANTON, DAVID L., "Cultural Confrontation in the Philippines," in *Cultural Frontiers of the Peace Corps*, ed. Robert B. Textor. Cambridge, Mass.: The M.I.T. Press, 1966.

THOMLINSON, RALPH, *Population Dynamics*. New York: Random House, Inc., 1965.

THORNDIKE, EDWARD L., *Your City*. New York: Harcourt Brace Jovanovich Inc., 1939.

U.S. DEPARTMENT OF LABOR, *The Negroes in the United States*. Washington, D.C.: Government Printing Office, 1966.

Bibliography

73